# RIGHTING CANADA'S
# WRONGS

## The Chinese Head Tax
## and Anti-Chinese Immigration Policies
## in the Twentieth Century

Arlene Chan

JAMES LORIMER & COMPANY LTD., PUBLISHERS
TORONTO

James Lorimer & Company Ltd., Publishers
acknowledges the support of the Ontario Arts
Council. We acknowledge the financial support of
the Government of Canada through the Canada
Book Fund for our publishing activities. We
acknowledge the support of the Canada Council
for the Arts which last year invested $24.3 million
in writing and publishing throughout Canada. We
acknowledge the Government of Ontario through
the Ontario Media Development Corporation's
Ontario Book Initiative.

Cover design: Tyler Cleroux

Library and Archives Canada Cataloguing in
Publication

Chan, Arlene, author
     The Chinese head tax and anti-Chinese
immigration policies in the
twentieth century / Arlene Chan.

(Righting Canada's wrongs)
Includes bibliographical references and index.
ISBN 978-1-4594-0443-4 (bound)

     1. Chinese--Taxation--Canada--History--
20th century--Juvenile literature.  2. Chinese--Legal
status, laws, etc.--Canada--History--20th century-
-Juvenile literature.  3. Emigration and immigration
law--
Canada--History--20th century--Juvenile literature.
4. Race discrimination--Canada--History--20th
century--Juvenile literature.  5. Chinese Canadians-
-History--20th century--Juvenile literature.  6.
Canada--Ethnic relations--History--20th century--
Juvenile literature.
I. Title.  II. Series: Righting Canada's wrongs

FC106.C5C47 2014          j971.004'951
C2014-903031-2

James Lorimer & Company Ltd., Publishers
317 Adelaide Street West, Suite 1002
Toronto, ON, Canada
M5V 1P9
www.lorimer.ca

Printed and bound in Canada.
Manufactured by Friesens Corporation in Altona,
Manitoba, Canada in August 2014.
Job # 205964

*To James Pon, Charlie Quan, and Gim Wong who all passed away during the writing
of this book and whose stories will be remembered and shared for generations to come.*

# Acknowledgements

*My deepest appreciation is extended to many individuals, families, and
organizations for their co-operation and enthusiasm in the massive undertaking
of collecting stories, photographs, and documents. I especially thank the unsung
heroes whose family stories about the hardships endured during the years of
the head tax and exclusionary period are featured. Thank you to the following
individuals, all of whose stories each merit an entire book: Albert Lee; Judi
Michelle Young; Germaine Wong; Sid Chow Tan; James and Vera Pon; Walter
Tom; Charlie Quan and his grandson, Terry Quan; Gim Wong and his son Jeff
Wong and daughter Donna Wong Malthus; Fung Hi Tom and her son, Matt
Eng; and Hank Wong and his son, Rick Wong.*

*I applaud the dedication of archivists, librarians, and historians without whom
the rich resources of archival materials would not otherwise have been available
for the successful completion of this book. I thank the following organizations:
Vancouver Public Library; Royal BC Museum; BC Archives; Ontario Archives;
Chinese Canadian Military Museum; Glenbow Archives; City of Toronto
Archives; City of Vancouver Archives; Manitoba Historical Society; Library of
Congress; Library and Archives Canada; McCord Museum; Newfoundland
and Labrador Head Tax Redress Organization; Vancouver Archives; Simon
Fraser University; City of St. John's Archives; University of British Columbia;
Saltwater City Television Collective; BC Coalition of Head Tax Payers; Head
Tax Families Society of Canada; Multicultural History Society of Ontario; and
Chinese Canadian National Council. Many individuals granted generous access
to their family photos and treasures. These include Jim Rosenthal, Keith Lock,
Pamelia Lock, Mavis Lew, Cheuk Kwan, Anthony Chan, Elwin Xie, Alfie Yip,
Bradley Lee, Shan Qiao, Victor Wong, Nelson Wong, Wynnie Chou, and Valerie
Mah. Thanks also to David H. T. Wong for permission to include an excerpt from
his graphic novel.*

*Lastly, I wish to acknowledge my family, especially my husband and sounding
board, Leo, and my sister, Janet, as well as Pam Hickman, whose guidance has
been unwavering.*

*— Arlene Chan*

# Contents

▶ **WATCH THE VIDEO**

Look for this symbol throughout the book for links to video and audio clips available online.

Visit www.lorimer.ca/wrongs to see the entire series

# Introduction

Over 225 years ago, fifty Chinese arrived in 1788 on the western shores of a land that came to be known as Canada. They hailed from China, a country boasting 5,000 years of civilization, rich with culture, inventions, and flourishing trade. Not until 1858, however, did the first major wave of Chinese arrive. Thousands of almost exclusively young men crossed the ocean to escape poverty and starvation in China and seek their fortunes in a faraway place they knew as Gold Mountain. These Chinese immigrants left behind wives, children, and other family members at great sacrifice, out of desperation to mine for riches.

At the outset, British Columbia paid little attention to the influx of Chinese. They worked as gold prospectors, then as labourers to dig ditches and build roads for a growing colony of the British Commonwealth. They found work in domestic and laundry services that were traditionally considered women's work. Chinese were at the bottom of the social and economic ladder, an unenviable spot that was shared by other Asians.

British Columbia became the sixth province of Canada with a promise that sealed the deal. A transcontinental railway would be built to join the newest province with the rest of Canada. The second wave of Chinese immigrants arrived in 1881 to fill a pressing need for railway workers. Seventeen thousand Chinese workers were employed and the railway was completed in 1885.

As vital as the Chinese were in the realization of Canada's nation-building from sea to sea, a series of anti-Chinese legislation was enacted to deal with the "Yellow Peril" that threatened the Canadian way of life.

Politicians, citizens, and the media advanced their visions for a "white Canada." A head tax was levied in 1885 on all Chinese immigrants, the only racial group to be subjected to such an entry fee. The intention was to discourage further Chinese immigration and prevent family life. Substantial increases of the head tax were implemented from $50 to $100 in 1900, then to $500 in 1903.

When the First World War broke out, the Chinese were excluded from conscription into the Canadian Armed Forces. Despite this, several hundred Chinese voluntarily enlisted with the hopes of gaining the right to vote and becoming accepted as fellow citizens. However, five years after the war, the Canadian government enacted the *Chinese Immigration Act* in 1923. The head tax had failed to stem the influx of Chinese as intended. Now the entry door into Canada was slammed shut for virtually all Chinese. Thousands of men were left stranded in Canada without their wives and children.

Against all odds, the Chinese in Canada struggled an uphill battle to be given the right to vote and to be treated fairly as equals, ultimately making Canada a better country. There were moments in history when the Chinese challenged racism with labour strikes in the mines and at railway construction sites, and protests during the Great Depression. For the most part, they suffered in silence as second-class citizens and retreated into Chinatowns across the country.

When Canada declared war on Japan during the Second World War, Canada and China shared a common enemy — Japan. The victorious end of the war in 1945 marked a milestone in Chinese-Canadian history. The attitude of Canadians changed for the better. In 1947, the *Chinese Immigration Act* was repealed and the right to vote was granted. More and more Chinese Canadians applied successfully for citizenship. By 1967, all anti-Chinese clauses were removed from Canada's immigration laws.

Chinese communities began rebuilding and revitalizing with the influx of immigrants, not only from China, but from Hong Kong, Taiwan, Vietnam, and other places around the world. As much as there was growing success among the Chinese-Canadian population in all walks of life and business, the community drive for an official apology and redress for the head tax and exclusionary period, called the head tax redress campaign, was drawn out for twenty-two years.

By the time Prime Minister Stephen Harper apologized in 2006, only a handful of head tax payers and their spouses had lived long enough to hear the apology and receive symbolic payments of compensation.

The surviving men and women who suffered during the head tax and exclusionary era are now seniors, respectfully referred to as *loh wah kew*. Many refuse to talk about the past; others, like the eight Chinese Canadians in this book, have come forward to share their stories, which paint a grim picture of how they and their families were affected by the head tax and the twenty-four years of Chinese exclusion.

Albert Lee's grandfather and father each paid the $500 head tax. Albert's father was the first Chinese boy to live in Halifax. He returned to China to get married, but his young wife was not allowed to return to Canada with him. They were separated for fifteen years until her arrival in Canada with a daughter he had never met. They had three more children, including Albert, born to parents who were old enough to be their grandparents.

Judi Michelle Young's father was among the first shipload of Chinese workers hired to build the Canadian Pacific Railway. Although he was among the few Chinese who had been granted citizenship, her father paid the head tax three times when he returned to Canada from his trips to China.

Gim Wong's father paid the $500 head tax and worked thirteen years before he could afford another head tax to bring Gim's mother. At the age of eighty-two, Gim did the unthinkable. He rode his motorcycle across Canada to bring attention to the head tax redress campaign.

Sid Chow Tan came to Canada as a one-year-old. Growing up in the only Chinese family in Battleford, Saskatchewan, he learned that he was a "paper son" whose grandparents lived in constant fear that their adopted son would be discovered and deported as an illegal immigrant. His grandparents were separated by the *Chinese Immigration Act* for twenty-five years, a family history that pushed Sid to the forefront of the head tax redress campaign.

James Pon's father paid $500 each for his wife and five-year-old son, James. It took seventeen years for his father to repay the loan. James kept the head tax a secret from his children and wife, Vera, out of shame and guilt. Despite a life of hardship, James became a decorated engineer as well as the co-founder with Vera of the Foundation to Commemorate the Chinese Railroad Workers in Canada.

Walter Tom's grandfather paid the $500 head tax and Walter's father was a paper son. Walter, who arrived in Quebec City as a toddler, did not know about his family history until he became an activist in the head tax redress campaign.

Germaine Wong's father was a head tax payer whose first wife died in China after years of separation from her husband. He remarried at the age of sixty-five but could not bring his wife and young daughter to Montreal until the repeal of the *Chinese Immigration Act*.

Fung Hi Tom married Wing Nun Eng, who paid the $300 head tax when he arrived in Newfoundland, a British colony at the time. As the surviving spouse of a head tax payer, Fung Hi received the symbolic compensation.

These are their stories.

# FROM CHINA TO CANADA

# Leaving China

Canada is a land of immigrants and all Canadians, with the exception of the Aboriginal peoples, are immigrants or descendants of immigrants. Newcomers escaped war, starvation, poverty, natural disasters, political upheavals, heavy taxes, and foreign occupation in their homelands. Adverse conditions such as these pushed them out of their countries and pulled them to a new land of hopes and dreams. These were the reasons for the Chinese to leave China, especially from Guangdong province in the south.

### Poverty Strikes All Ages
Poverty was a fact of life for farmers young and old, as seen in this photo from 1870. Rice fields were handed down from generation to generation or rented from landowners who collected a share of the crops as payment, but there was only enough farmland in Guangdong province to feed one-third of its population.

### Too Many People
By the mid-1800s, Chinese people began leaving their country in large numbers to look for work. The population had reached 420 million, having tripled in 300 years. These men and boys, pictured in 1909, faced unemployment and poverty, with few prospects.

**Ancestral Homes**

Chinese farmers typically lived in villages with homes of mud brick and sloping roofs, like these ones shown in 1918. They were born, married, and buried there, some dying without ever venturing far from home. Loyalty to their villages was strong, a bond deeply ingrained even after generations of living elsewhere.

**Too Little for Too Many**

Between 1780 and 1850, the population of Guangdong province increased from 16 million to 28 million. Although this was an important agricultural region of China, the rapid growth resulted in starvation and poverty due to the shortage of farmland.

**Faces of Starvation**

China has a long history of famine, averaging close to one annually for the last 2,000 years. Millions of Chinese have died from starvation, despite famine relief from countries like the US in the early 1900s.

Leaving China

## Foreign Occupation

The Empress Dowager, regarded as one of the most formidable women in history, ruled China with an iron fist, but even she could not save her country from its downfall. China was unable to quell uprisings against her government. The Sino-Japanese War in 1894 resulted in Taiwan being handed to Japan. The loss of the Opium Wars led to the capture of the capital city, Beijing. China was forced to open its ports for trading and to bear the shame of giving up Hong Kong to Britain. Other countries, including Germany and France, began occupying China. After years of restricting the intrusion of outsiders, China was being taken over by foreign countries that established their control in major cities, like Shanghai. China was being cut to pieces by Western and Japanese powers.

## Natural Disasters Wreak Havoc

Between 1851 and 1908 Guangdong province endured fourteen floods, seven typhoons, four earthquakes, two droughts, four plagues, and five famines. Chinese soldiers distributed food rations in 1909.

## Living Conditions

This page from the graphic novel *Escape to Gold Mountain* illustrates some of the push factors for the Chinese to leave China. The taxes were high and families faced starvation. The majority of farmers, most of them deeply in debt, rented farmland from landlords. Many uprisings brought death to over 20 million people, as warlords and their armies fought for power and bandits raided villages for food.

Chapter 1: From China to Canada

## Fall from Greatness

During the Qing dynasty (1644–1911), China was ruled by the Manchus, people from the northeastern part of the country who were regarded as outsiders by the overwhelmingly Han Chinese people. By adopting the Chinese form of government and retaining its officials, the Manchus governed with unchallenged authority. Beginning in the mid-1800s, after centuries of being advanced in trading, the arts, and sciences, China suffered through uprisings, a declining economy, population growth, and insufficient food supplies. Foreign countries were expanding their empires — Britain in India, France in Vietnam, Russia in lands north of China. With the country's fortunes misspent and overspent, the financial hardships fell upon its citizens, with high taxes. Adding to this burden, the Chinese became second-class citizens in their own country as foreign countries established their domination.

## Across the Ocean

Almost all of the people who left China came from a small number of counties in Guangdong province. The Chinese who went to the New World came from even fewer counties in the same province. They travelled from their villages to Hong Kong, where they boarded ships to cross the Pacific Ocean. Emigrants from China are known as "overseas Chinese."

China
Guangdong

Canada

### Guangdong

Sanshui
Panyu
Zengcheng
Nanhai
Dongguang
Heshan
Shunde
Kaiping
Baoan
Xinhui
Zhongshan
Enping
Taishan

Three Counties
Four Counties
Four Counties

CHINA

**GUANGDONG Province**

**Four Counties (Si Yi)**

Kaiping
Xinhui
Enping
Taishan

## Counties of Origin

In 1672, laws banned travel outside of China, except by special permit, until the 1860s. The early Chinese immigrants who came to Canada were poor, illiterate farmers, mainly from two areas — San Yi (three counties of Nanhai, Panyu, and Shunde) and Si Yi (four counties of Taishan, Xinhui, Kaiping, and Enping). Many had little to no working experience beyond farming.

# Early Chinese Immigrants

Although there is evidence of Buddhist monks arriving over one thousand years earlier, 1788 is recorded as the date of the first Chinese to set foot on a land that was to be called Canada.

Not until 1858 did Chinese immigrants arrive in large numbers. Gold was discovered in the Fraser Valley in British Columbia, a colony of the British Commonwealth. Thousands of Chinese arrived from California, where they had mined the gold rush of 1848. Soon afterwards, they were followed by boatloads of fortune-seekers from China.

The destination, whether it was California or BC, was *Gum Shan*, meaning Gold Mountain. At first, this was the name of a faraway place in North America where gold had been discovered. Eventually, Gold Mountain became the name for any place that fuelled the dream of attaining riches.

### All for Fur

Captain John Meares arrived by ship at Nootka Sound on Vancouver Island in 1788 with fifty Chinese labourers, carpenters, and shipbuilders to construct a trading post and schooner for the trade of sea otter furs. The high quality and beauty of this fur made it the most valuable and sought after pelt in Chinese trade. Sea otter fur, a sign of wealth and status, was worn as belts, capes, and trim on silk robes. After being driven out by Spanish traders, many of the Chinese settled on the island and raised families with First Nations women.

### Along the River

A junk, or Chinese sailboat, navigates the Pearl River, China's third largest river, as it flows through Guangdong province. The area surrounding the river delta was the largest source of Chinese immigrants to Canada until the 1970s. The New World beckoned with stories of gold, wealth, and riches. The dream was to work hard overseas and retire to the homeland. The reality was that most Chinese who went overseas did not return to China.

**Dreaming of Gold**

The discovery of gold in California marked one of the most significant American historical events. Thousands of gold miners travelled over land, across the mountains, and by sea in 1848. Chinese were among the many prospectors who were lured to California by word of mouth and by pamphlets distributed by ship owners selling tickets for the voyage overseas. Upon their arrival, the Chinese worked on sites that had been abandoned by white miners. They were accepted until the gold finds became scarcer.

**Easy to Pick On**

Even though these American and Chinese miners worked a claim side by side in California in 1852, the Chinese camps were segregated from the rest of the miners. Chinese were easy targets when the gold rush was nearing an end and the anti-foreign movement in the US began. Decreasing gold finds and increasing unemployment led to claims that the Chinese were taking away jobs and working at lower wages. In 1850, a tax of twenty dollars a month was charged to all foreign miners.

Early Chinese Immigrants

## Perils of Panning

Two gold rushes, one after the other, brought thousands of gold seekers to BC. The Fraser Gold Rush (1858–1863) crowded the shores of the Fraser River with prospectors. Later, the Cariboo Gold Rush (1860–1863) drew thousands farther north. Miners used simple tools to sift gold from the riverbanks. The Chinese were treated poorly — forced from mining sites, robbed, beaten, and even murdered. They avoided the paths of white miners.

## So Unlike the Others

Chinese miners, like this one with his shoulder pole and modest mining equipment of pickaxe and shovel, stood out from the white miners. They spoke an unfamiliar language, ate with strange-looking implements called chopsticks, and wore odd-looking jackets with cloth buttons. Their long black hair was tied back in braids, or queues, a hairstyle required by law in China. Any man who cut off his braid was executed for the crime of treason against the Manchu government.

Chapter 1: From China to Canada

### Transporting Goods
A man balances two baskets with a shoulder pole made of wood or bamboo. This traditional method of transporting goods, still commonly used in China, was used for carrying supplies and moving rock debris for construction projects. In Vancouver, a bylaw was passed to forbid the selling of vegetables brought into town with shoulder poles.

### Canada's First Chinatown
Within two years of the Fraser Gold Rush, Victoria, B.C. grew from a population of 300 to a community of 1,577 Chinese and 2,884 white residents. The first Chinatown in Canada was established there. For fifty years (1858–1910) it was the largest one in Canada, and the second largest for almost forty years (1911–1950). It remains the only Canadian Chinatown that dates from the first arrival of Chinese immigrants to the present day.

# Why Canada?

Canada is a vast country, abundant with forests, fish, land, and furs. In 1867, Canada was in its infancy as a country, a new confederation of the four eastern provinces of Ontario, Quebec, New Brunswick, and Nova Scotia. As farmlands were soon filled to capacity, the government looked to the west, with its expanse of land. The foundations of British Columbia, a British colony on the Pacific coast, were being laid, necessitating an influx of labourers. Moreover, more settlers were needed there to safeguard it from the threat of an American takeover. Although only immigrants of British and European heritage were desired there, Chinese men whose dreams of getting rich during the gold rush were unfulfilled found employment as labourers.

### Settling the West
Wheat farming established its economic importance after Confederation. To this end, the government implemented immigration policies and vigorous campaigns to attract settlers from Europe and the US to populate and farm the prairies. Pamphlets and posters were distributed. Ship passage was subsidized and railway fares were reduced. Free land was offered. By 1914, over a million settlers had arrived on the Prairies.

### Forests Advance Canada
With more than one-and-a-half million square kilometres of timberland, Canada ranks third as a producer of wood and lumber. Wood was the staple of Canadian trade during the nineteenth century, and it attracted investments and immigrants.

### Workers Needed

Manpower for labour-intensive jobs, like the construction of the Great Western Railway in Ontario, was needed. Chinese labourers were hired to fill this need by building roads and bridges, digging ditches, stringing telegraph wires, draining swamps, clearing land, and working in fish canneries and coal mines.

### Life as a Logger

The logging industry was vital for the construction of homes, buildings, ships, and railroads. Chinese workers cleared forests so the land could be settled by the influx of white immigrants. They were hired to work in logging camps, like the MacInnes lumber camp in Elkmouth, BC, where trees were cut down by hand and dragged to a lake or river to move the timber by water.

### Life at a Rice Mill

A Chinese worker, seen here at the Victoria Rice Mill in 1889, had responsibility for removing the husk and bran from the grain kernels to produce white rice.

Why Canada?

# Canadian Society at the Turn of the Century

Until the 1850s, the majority of immigrants who arrived in British North America were British subjects. When Canada was born as a nation in 1867, it became a proud member of the vast empire of the British Commonwealth, which included India, Australia, New Zealand, the South Pacific, and large parts of Africa. The British Union Jack was the Canadian flag and "God Save the Queen" was the national anthem. As a British colony, Canada was white Anglo-Saxon Protestant. The vision for Canada was a "white man's country."

**Victoria as a Name**
The town of Victoria, illustrated in 1862 during the gold rush, was named after Queen Victoria and made the seat of government. Established in 1843 as a fort for the Hudson's Bay Company, it transformed from a quiet English village to a bustling centre with several streets, a few hundred stores, and several thousand residents. Victoria's British ancestry runs strong today, with its double-decker buses, horse-drawn carriages, tearooms, and expansive gardens. No individual has been more honoured than Queen Victoria in the naming of public buildings, streets, and places, with her name appearing over 300 times on the map of Canada.

**Sixty-Four Years a Queen**
Queen Victoria ruled the British Commonwealth for sixty-four years, from 1837 to 1901. The British Empire covered one-fifth of the earth's surface and ruled one-quarter of its people. Her tastes, values, and behaviour set the standard for her British subjects, including Canadians. After her death in 1901, Canada established a national public holiday, Victoria Day, in honour of her birthday. She is regarded as the "Mother of Confederation."

Chapter 1: From China to Canada

## Victorian Society

The government, educators, and citizens instilled British values and patriotism in a Victorian society that was distinctly Christian. A high value was placed on morality. Children were educated to be as British as possible and school books were filled with British references.

## Canada's Flag

The Union Jack, the national flag of Britain, was first raised in Canada in 1610 and adopted as Canada's national symbol and flag in 1904 to show allegiance as a member of the British Commonwealth. Above, Union Jack flags are prominently displayed for a parade in Ottawa. The current national flag, with its red-white-red bars and central maple leaf, was proclaimed by Queen Elizabeth II in 1965.

## British Royalty

Canada's identity remained closely tied to Britain even after Queen Victoria's death. Royal visits were widely popular and reinforced Canada's patriotic feelings for the British Commonwealth. Hastings Street in Vancouver was decorated with Union Jacks during the visit of King George VI and Queen Elizabeth in 1939.

Canadian Society at the Turn of the Century

# LIFE IN CANADA, 1860s–1900

# Experiencing Racism

Anti-Chinese discrimination has its roots in China. As far back as the Ming dynasty (1368–1644), the Chinese controlled trade with foreigners and limited them to ports like Hong Kong and Macau. Beginning in the mid-1800s, however, foreign countries moved into the interior and other ports. Cities like Shanghai were divided into French, American, British, and Japanese concessions, or sectors, where Chinese laws did not apply. Unable to halt foreign occupation, China became regarded as a weak and inferior nation. Any Chinese who went overseas were treated with as much disdain and disrespect as their homeland.

**Legislated Racism**

Between 1878 and 1899, the government passed twenty-six laws to restrict the Chinese as much as possible. Racist laws, regulations, and policies against them soon exceeded one hundred. This sidewalk sign in Vancouver rallied white males to vote, a right denied to the "Mongolian and Chinese race" due to their lack of "British instincts or British feelings or aspirations."

**Political Cartoon**

This 1879 political cartoon shows a "heathen Chinee" having his queue pulled by Amor De Cosmos, who later served as the second premier of BC. By 1881, there were 4,383 Chinese in the province — 99 per cent of all Chinese in Canada — where anti-Chinese sentiment was the most severe.

### It's All Their Fault

After the gold rush ended, jobs were hard to find. The Chinese were singled out as unfair job seekers, because they worked for lower wages, lived more cheaply in rundown homes, and had no families to support and feed in Canada. They were also accused of not contributing financially to the country's economy, because they sent their earnings to China instead of spending their money in Canada. Blaming the Chinese for problems in BC became a powerful tool for citizens, politicians, and the media to keep them isolated socially, economically, and politically.

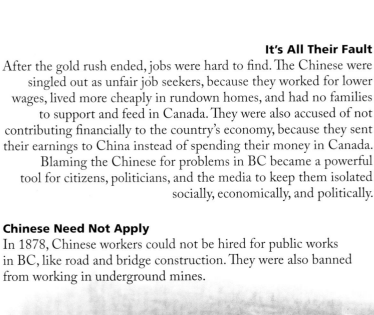

### Chinese Need Not Apply

In 1878, Chinese workers could not be hired for public works in BC, like road and bridge construction. They were also banned from working in underground mines.

### Naturalization

Anyone who wanted to become a British subject had to petition the courts — a process called naturalization. Judges had the power to reject requests. In 1899, Judi Michelle Young's father, Yong Hong Yan was among the less than 5 per cent of Chinese who were naturalized.

Judi Michelle Young:
> "[Naturalization] was extremely rare at that time . . . He thought it meant Canadian citizenship . . . but it really meant very little."

Experiencing Racism

# Building the Railway

When BC joined Canada, Prime Minister John A. Macdonald promised a trans-Canada railway to join the newest province with the rest of the country. The land between Port Moody and Eagle Pass was mountainous, making the railway project challenging and dangerous. BC had no more than 400 men available for such work. Between 1881 and 1884, 17,000 Chinese men were recruited to work on the railway. They received a daily wage of one dollar that paid for their food, equipment, and lodging. White workers did not have to pay for these expenses and had higher daily wages of $1.50 to $2.50.

**Labourers Needed**
Despite strong objections from citizens, politicians, and labour organizations, Prime Minister John A. Macdonald approved the hiring of Chinese labourers for the construction of the Canadian Pacific Railway (CPR). "Either you must have this labour or you cannot have the railway." As much as Chinese workers were deeply resented, they were nonetheless desperately needed.

**Chinese Railway Workers**
Andrew Onderdonk, an American contractor who was hired for the project, had experience in the US with Chinese railway workers. Much to the dismay of the citizens and politicians of BC, he proposed their hiring. The Workingmen's Protection Association unsuccessfully petitioned the government to not use "Mongolian labour."

Either you must have this labour or you cannot have the railway.

## Work in Gold Mountain

Recruiters signed up workers in China. Eager to go to Gold Mountain, thousands made their way to the port of Hong Kong. For the ship fare, some borrowed money from their relatives or fellow villagers. Others signed contracts and borrowed money from the recruitment contractors. Many were only in their early teens, young boys who usually found work as tea boys serving tea for the railway workers.

## Desperate Times

Judi Michelle Young's father and his brothers were among the first railway recruits. "China was going through a very difficult famine . . . they had to leave the country one way or another."

🔊 Listen to Judi Michelle Young talk about her father's employment with the CPR at www.tinyurl.com/rcwheadtax01.

**LISTEN TO THE AUDIO**

## All Aboard

These young Chinese men are aboard a CPR ship en route to Canada. They were ill-prepared for the harsh Canadian winters in their light cotton pants and cotton footwear. For up to two months, they endured the voyage from Hong Kong to Victoria, BC, tossed by the waves of the Pacific Ocean. Seasick, miserable, and alone among strangers, they lived below deck, shoulder to shoulder, knee to knee, in cramped conditions with closed hatches and bad ventilation. The only times that they had fresh air was during their meal times of rationed rice and tea.

James Pon:
    "[My grandfather] said, 'First
    I'll go to Canada and work on
    the railroad, then I'll go to
    Gold Mountain to pan for gold.'
    My grandfather knew of the
    dangers involved because some
    of the villagers who had gone
    to Gold Mountain had never been
    heard from again."

Building the Railway

### Far From Family

James Pon's grandfather, Pon Hincheng, who was born in Taishan, Guangdong province, left his family to work on the construction of the CPR. After its completion, he was forced to stay in Vancouver because he couldn't afford the ship passage home. He had sent his savings to his family in China. By the early 1900s, he had saved $200 from his earnings running a laundry to bring over two of his sons, including James's father, Soon Long Pon.

James Pon:

> "He was far from his family
> . . . faced hostile sentiments
> and worked night and day to make
> completion of the railway possible."

### Railway Camp

Chinese workers were segregated into camps, like this one in Kamloops, BC. After a section of the railway track was completed, they dismantled their tents and moved on foot to the new work section, often over forty kilometres away.

### From San Francisco

Sid Chow Tan's great-grandfather, Chow Sing Tan, came to BC from San Francisco and brought along his son, Chow Sing, to work as a labourer for the CPR.

Sid Chow Tan:

> "My grandfather [Chow Sing] was brought to
> Canada in 1919 by my great-uncle. That uncle
> worked on the railway, and his father who
> brought him over to work on the railway was
> here during the California Gold Rush."

Chapter 2: Life In Canada, 1860s-1900

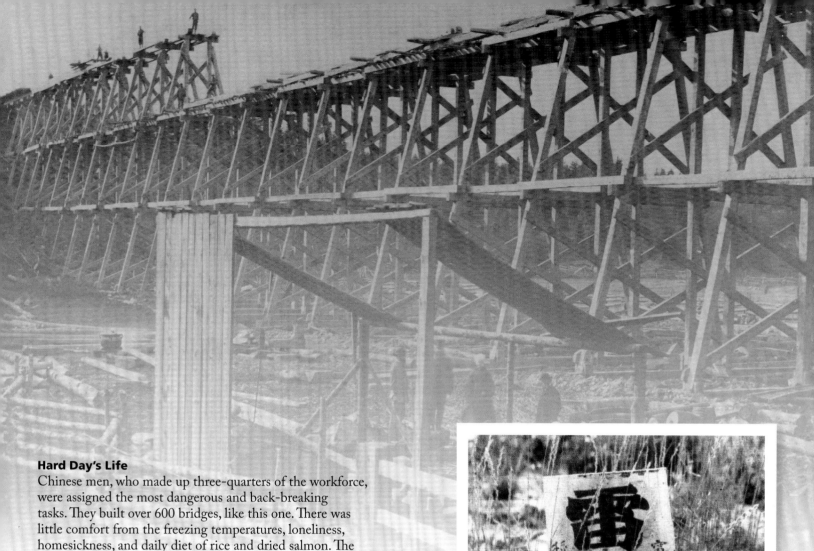

**Hard Day's Life**

Chinese men, who made up three-quarters of the workforce, were assigned the most dangerous and back-breaking tasks. They built over 600 bridges, like this one. There was little comfort from the freezing temperatures, loneliness, homesickness, and daily diet of rice and dried salmon. The lack of fresh vegetables and fruit contributed to malnutrition.

**Ultimate Sacrifice**

Hundreds of Chinese workers died due to accidents, explosions, cold weather, rock slides, cave-ins, illness, harsh living conditions, scurvy, and malnutrition. An estimated 600 Chinese died — one for every mile of railway track — although actual figures are likely higher.

**No Chinese Invited**

On November 7, 1885, at 9:22 a.m., the western and central sections of the transcontinental railway were officially joined at Craigellachie, BC. The driving of the last spike is the greatest symbol of Canada's unity. The motto, *A Mari usque ad Mare*, refers to a country joined from sea to sea, the Atlantic to the Pacific Oceans. The CPR, completed six years ahead of schedule, would not have been built without Chinese labourers; however, none were invited to this historic event.

Building the Railway

# The Head Tax

From the moment of the driving of the last spike in 1885, Canada turned its back on the Chinese. With a failing economy in BC and thousands jobless, they became scapegoats for the unemployment problems. In 1885, a public enquiry, the Royal Commission on Chinese Immigration, gathered information on how to deal with the "Chinese question." It resulted in the first anti-Chinese immigration law, *An Act to Restrict and Regulate Chinese Immigration into Canada*. A $50 head tax was to be paid by Chinese immigrants, the only group singled out by racial origin in this manner. The intention was to discourage any more Chinese from coming to Canada and bringing their wives and children. The average Chinese labourer earned $225 a year and saved only $43 after paying for food, clothing, rent, and other living expenses. The $50 head tax was a heavy financial burden.

## The intention was to discourage any more Chinese from coming to Canada and bringing their wives and children.

**Foreigners Not Suitable**

The Royal Commission on Chinese Immigration reported that the Chinese were a public menace to Canada's social and moral life. While a handful of witnesses, like the Chinese Consul General, spoke in favour of the Chinese, the majority viewed them as "perpetual foreigners." "I do not think that it would be to the advantage of Canada or any other country occupied by Aryans for members of the Mongolian race to become permanent inhabitants of the country," said Prime Minister Macdonald.

Chapter 2: Life In Canada, 1860s-1900

RT

MISSION

MIGRATION.

EVIDENCE.

WA:
OF THE COMMISSION.

35

---

**Tax payable by Chinese immigrants.**

**6.** Every person of Chinese origin, irrespective of allegiance, shall pay into the Consolidated Revenue Fund of Canada, on entering Canada, at the port or place of entry, a tax of five hundred dollars, except the following persons who shall be exempt from such payment, that is to say :—

**Exemptions.**

(*a.*) The members of the Diplomatic Corps, or other Government representatives, their suites and their servants, and consuls and consular agents;

(*b.*) The children born in Canada of parents of Chinese origin who have left Canada for educational or other purposes, on substantiating their identity to the satisfaction of the controller at the port or place where they seek to enter on their return ;

(*c.*) Merchants, their wives and children, the wives and children of clergymen, tourists, men of science and students, who shall substantiate their status to the satisfaction of the controller, subject to the approval of the Minister, or who are bearers of certificates of identity, specifying their occupation and their object in coming into Canada, or other similar documents issued by the Government or by a recognized official or representative of the Government whose subjects they are ;

(*d.*) In the case of a person of Chinese origin who is the personal attendant or servant of a British subject visiting Canada, the tax payable under the first subsection of this section may be refunded to the person paying the same, upon his furnishing satisfactory evidence that such Chinese attendant or servant is leaving the port of entry with his employer or master, on his return to China, if within twelve months of the date of his arrival in Canada, and upon returning to the controller of such port the certificate granted under section 13.

**Certificate proving exemption.**

2. Every such certificate or other document shall be in the English or French language, and shall be examined and

106                                                                   endorsed

## Head Tax

The $50 head tax drastically reduced Chinese immigrants from thousands to 212 in 1886. Although the head tax, later increased to $100, then $500, was deliberately set to deter immigration, the push factors to leave China were so strong that the numbers climbed back up. Even a strongly worded flyer from a Chinese organization in Victoria failed to discourage them. "There are now about 20,000 Chinese in Canada who are unemployed . . . They can get no work . . . to save themselves from cold and starvation."

# Every person of Chinese origin, irrespective of allegiance, shall pay . . . on entering Canada, at the port or place of entry, a tax of five hundred dollars . . .

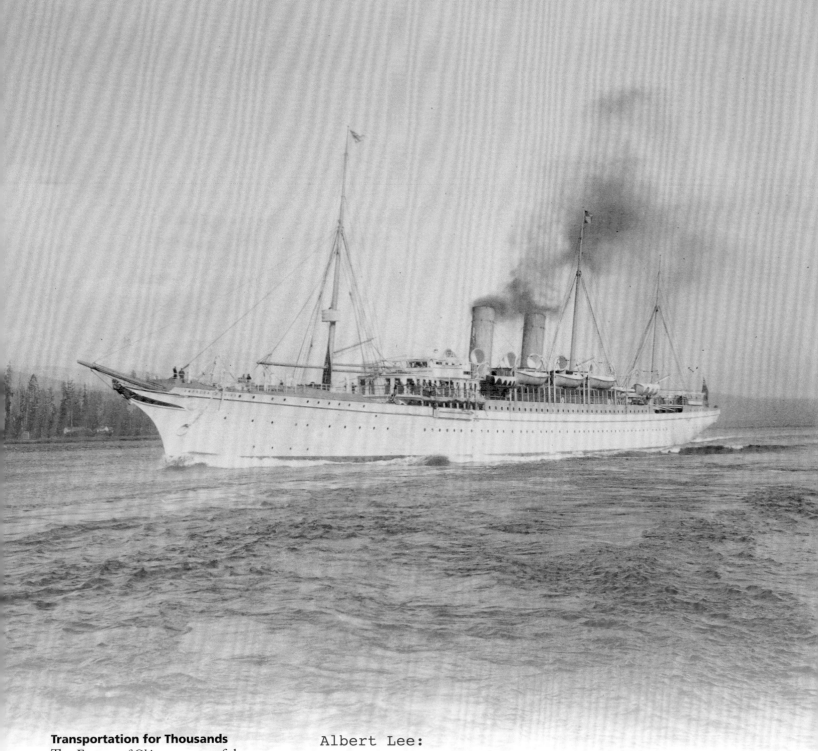

**Transportation for Thousands**

The *Empress of China* was one of the Canadian Pacific class of ocean liners that transported thousands of immigrants across the Pacific Ocean beginning in 1891. There were three generations of *Empress* liners that were also used to deliver mail, silk, and tea. Although these luxury ships dominated first-class travel across the Pacific, the Chinese travelled as third-class passengers below deck in steerage.

Albert Lee:

"My grandfather arrived in 1906 and he had left the village by ox cart through mountains and [by] crossing rivers. It took a week or so to arrive in Hong Kong and then he would have stockpiled some food and supplies for a three-week voyage across the Pacific Ocean. Once he arrived in Vancouver, he would go to Chinatown and stock up again. It would take another week or ten days to take the train right across Vancouver to Halifax."

Destitute, no fuel, no food,
we borrow money to go abroad.
No matter what we say or do,
The customs men won't let us through.
Like convicts, locked up in some
      island cell,
We rail against this unjust hell.

Many poems, like this one, were carved
on the walls of the immigration centre
to express feelings of frustration,
shame, and disbelief at being locked
up like criminals.

# After ships landed in BC, passengers were taken to the prison-like immigration centre for processing.

**Pig House**

After ships landed in BC, passengers were taken to the prison-like immigration centre for processing, including a medical examination, and secured in rooms with windows covered by iron screens and bars. Charlie Quan remembers being "locked up like a pig in a cage" for one month and being humiliated in what came to be known by the Chinese as the pig house. Immigration officials forced him to stand naked for half an hour "for really no reason at all."

The Head Tax

# A Working Life

Unemployed railway workers needed to find new jobs. Barbers, butchers, and café owners, who relied on selling their services to the railway workforce, lost their businesses too. Several thousand Chinese returned to China; however, many more could not afford to buy the return ship fare that had been promised to them by Andrew Onderdonk. They stayed in BC where they found work as coal miners, farm labourers, gardeners, grocers, cooks, or domestic servants. Others moved east, settling in towns and cities along the railway, and opening laundries, grocery stores, and cafés. Some worked in mines, on farms and cattle ranches as cooks, and wherever else work could be found.

**Logging in Demand**
As the demand for lumber grew, logging and sawmill operations, like the Hastings Sawmill in Strathcona, BC, were established in record numbers. Many Chinese and Japanese workers found employment in the logging industry, where they harvested timber and hauled it to the mills.

Chapter 2: Life In Canada, 1860s-1900

### Iron Chink

Chinese workers were needed for fish canneries, like this one in Nanaimo, because salmon was a valuable export of BC. The work was unpleasant and smelly, especially during the hot summer months. The fish were gutted and cut up, then packed, cooked, and sealed in cans. When a machine was invented to mechanize the process, it was named the "Iron Chink," after the Chinese workers it was designed to replace. The word "chink" is a racist, offensive term referring to someone of Chinese ethnicity. Gim Wong worked, as a nineteen-year-old, at a cannery on the Skeena River in BC. He was paid 17½ cents an hour while non-Chinese men earned 35 cents.

Gim Wong:

    "There was no negotiating. We accepted it. Every penny counted."

### Gulf of Georgia Cannery

In the early 1900s, 10,000 men, 6,000 of them Chinese, worked in canneries along the Pacific coast. The Japanese worked mostly as fishermen while the Chinese were employed exclusively in the fish canneries. Unless they were British citizens, the Chinese were not allowed to make their living from fishing. The Gulf of Georgia Cannery was the centre of BC's salmon fishery. Located in Steveston, where the second largest population of Japanese people lived, it was designated a National Historic Site of Canada to commemorate the history of Canada's west coast fishing industry.

## Coal Mining

Between 1881 and 1925, coal was the primary fuel of the Western world. The coal mines on Vancouver Island provided 50 per cent of Canada's coal exports and relied on Chinese workers. In 1986, a memorial was erected in Cumberland to commemorate the Chinese and Japanese miners who were killed in accidents.

## Women's Work

With the shortage of white and Chinese women, many Chinese men operated laundries to fill the demand for washing, ironing, and clothes mending. Laundries are the oldest Chinese business in Canada, the first one opening in 1861 in New Westminster, BC.

## Business Partnerships

The Yan War store in Barkerville, shown here in 1890, was operated by a partnership of several Chinese men. This business arrangement allowed the Chinese to pool their financial resources, provide work for themselves, hire their relatives, and avoid the discrimination of white employers.

## Grocery Stores

Vera Pon's mother, Ho See, worked at the family grocery store, similar to the Lim Gong one in Vancouver shown here, while raising her twelve children. Vera helped by preparing vegetables, taking orders, and delivering to the shops in Vernon, BC.

### More Than One Job

Judi Michelle Young's father, Yong Hong Yan, continued working for the CPR, likely due to his fluency in Chinese and English. "He roomed and boarded these new recruits at this particular spot in Mission City [BC] . . . probably just a general store [with] fruit [and] vegetables ,whatever he was able to support his family with at that time. There had to be some kind of augmentation."

### Travel By Train

The CPR increased the popularity of rail travel by promoting tourism in the Rocky Mountains and building luxury hotels, like Chateau Lake Louise in Alberta, for the tourists. Many Chinese were hired to work as cooks, boatmen, and bellboys.

TRAVEL
*Canadian Pacific*
ACROSS CANADA!

### A Cook's Life

Chinese cooks found work in homes, hotels, farms, ranches, restaurants, and logging camps, like this one. A typical day was spent preparing three meals, chopping wood for the fire, carrying water from the stream, feeding the pigs, and tending the kitchen garden.

A Working Life

# Chinese Life

The Chinese were connected by networks of tight-knit families, because great importance was placed on kinship as the foundation of society. Like the links of a chain, they migrated around the world to join relatives who sent money to bring them to a new country. Sons followed fathers, nephews followed uncles, cousins followed cousins. Through loyalty to their families, they relied on one another for companionship, finding jobs and places to live, and lending money to get settled. The definition of family extended beyond blood relations. People who shared the same surname or came from the same village were regarded as family members.

**Chee Kung Tong Association**
Barkerville was settled by prospectors during the Cariboo Gold Rush. By the 1880s, half of the town's population was Chinese. The earliest Chinese association was the Chee Kung Tong, later known as the Chinese Freemasons, which provided social welfare to the Chinese in need and fought against racism. By 1900, there were more than forty Chee Kung Tong associations in BC with an estimated membership of 10,000 to 20,000 in total. The building for the Chee Kung Tong in Barkerville was designated a National Historic Site of Canada in 2007.

Like the links of a chain, they migrated around the world to join relatives . . .

**Victoria**

Forced by circumstance, the Chinese sequestered themselves into close-knit communities, like this one in the outskirts of Victoria. White Canadians did not want the Chinese to live near them. These settlements came to be known as Chinatowns. Anti-Chinese racism justified segregation of the Chinese by municipal governments.

**Family Associations**

The Chinese relied on one another for help. They formed associations that provided services unavailable elsewhere, as well as a welcoming place to socialize and meet people. Membership, based on political, kinship, or regional affiliations, was the backbone of Chinese communities across Canada and provided an important link to the cultural traditions of their homeland. The Lung Kong Tin Yee family association (the Toronto chapter is shown here) is one of many such associations worldwide. Its members share the surnames of four military heroes (Liu, Guan, Zhang, and Zhao) from China's historical era of the Three Kingdoms (220–280).

## Political Associations

Some associations, like the Guomindang, were made up of members who shared the same political beliefs. In the early 1900s, political associations, like the Chinese Empire Reform Association, believed that China could be restored to its former prominence in the world by reforming the ruling Manchu monarchy. Others believed the government needed to be replaced with a republic. In 1911, the Manchus were overthrown and in 1912 the Guomindang became the ruling political party in the newly established Republic of China. The Guomindang held key political importance in Chinese communities in Canada until the early 1970s.

## Chinese Benevolent Association

The Chinese Benevolent Association, established in 1884, took on the role of a Chinese government in Canada and helped newcomers find places to work and live. It looked after unemployed, homeless, and sick people, and settled disputes and disagreements in the community. The organization played an important role in fighting anti-Chinese discrimination and unfair treatment by Canadians. Associations, like the one above in Victoria, typically were divided into a sleeping area, kitchen, social space, meeting hall, and altar room, shown on the right with flags, flowers, and incense.

# The organization played an important role in fighting anti-Chinese discrimination and unfair treatment by Canadians.

**Credit Service**
Chinese associations provided an essential banking service that operated like a credit union. Members pooled their money and helped one another borrow money, a system that benefited the borrowers, the lenders, and the associations.

**Chinese Music**
Religious beliefs, music, language, foods, and traditions were important ways of providing cultural links to China. The Chinese formed music clubs, like this church group in Victoria in 1892, and played traditional instruments. Chinese music was a popular pastime that provided much-needed relief from the daily drudgery of being in a hostile country.

### Chinese Opera

Chinese opera has been a beloved art form in China for over 800 years. While there are over 300 types of opera, the early Chinese enjoyed Cantonese opera because it was the popular form in their villages. Well-known tales of romance and history were brought to life on stage by performers in the roles of warriors, villains, and generals, as the orchestra accompanied them with traditional Chinese instruments.

### Lion Dance

The lion dance, as shown on the streets of Nanaimo, BC, is a tradition that dates back hundreds of years in China and figures prominently in Chinese celebrations and festivals. The lion symbolizes strength and courage, frightens away bad luck, and brings good fortune. Performed by martial artists, the lion dance is physically demanding due to its acrobatic and lively routines.

> . . . the early Chinese enjoyed Cantonese opera because it was the popular form in their villages. Well-known tales of romance and history were brought to life on stage . . .

# PREFACE.

THIS Reader contains nearly 1500 different words. The Dictionary contains all the words occuring in the Reader, and some 4600 additional, or more than 6000 in all. It also has over 1500 sentences illustrating the meaning of the words. The Chinese scholar will find most of the words in the Dictionary that he will ordinarily meet with in reading or speaking.

The lessons in the Reader are graded as slowly, as the limited space, and introduction of as many new words as possible, would allow. The lessons are on a variety of subjects, and include a great many sentences used in ordinary conversation. Gospel truths have been introduced as far as practicable throughout; and the design of the whole is, not only to lead the scholar into the knowledge of the English language, but also of the truth. The Chinese portion is in the Canton dialect, which is the spoken language of this people in America, Australia and the Sandwich Islands. The object of using this dialect instead of the more ~~~~~~~~~~~~ the learner ~~~~~~~~ and simple ~~~~~~~ expressing

I. M. C.

# ENGLISH AND CHINESE
# READER,

BY REV. I. M. CONDIT,
MISSIONARY TO THE CHINESE.

*Mr Chiu Hing*

# AMERICAN TRACT SOCIETY,
150 NASSAU STREET, NEW YORK.

上海美華書館銅板　英語入門　耶穌降世一千八百三十年

### Churches

This reader was published by an American missionary in 1882 to teach English and Chinese. Churches were very active in educating and supporting Chinese immigrants. They were among the few Canadian organizations that offered assistance to the Chinese in the early years of discrimination.

### Spreading the Word

Missionaries made great efforts to convert the Chinese to Christianity, not only in China but in Canada. Although Bibles were widely distributed, most Chinese could not read or write. The acceptance of Christianity did not necessarily mean that the converted abandoned their original religious beliefs. Rather, they often mixed the new faith with their traditional Chinese beliefs, including Buddhism, Daoism, and Confucianism.

Chinese Life

# Chinese Women in Canada

With few exceptions, only men left China to fill Canada's call for labourers. A mere handful of women came to Canada, limited not only by the prohibitive costs of the ship fare and head tax, but also by cultural tradition that required women to care for their husbands' parents and households. Limited in their social interactions and isolated by their gender and ethnicity, they raised their children without the support of an extended family that life in China would have offered. They often worked in their husbands' businesses.

**First Chinese Woman**
The first Chinese woman in Canada was Mrs. Kwong Lee, who arrived in Victoria in 1860. Early female arrivals were usually the wives or daughters of wealthy merchants. Her husband was a successful San Francisco store owner who expanded his business of selling Chinese goods to Vancouver. Gam Young, photographed in 1896, lived in Brockton, Ontario.

## So Few Women
By tradition, Chinese women were expected to stay at home and look after the children and their husbands' parents. In 1885, there were 10,335 Chinese men and only 157 Chinese women in Canada, a gender imbalance that was the most severe compared to other immigrant groups. In 1902, Victoria had a Chinese population of 3,283 with only 96 women. The low ratio of males to females was used as evidence that the Chinese had no intention of settling in Canada.

**LISTEN TO THE AUDIO**

## Read All About It
The arrival of Lock Quong's wife was front-page news in the *Toronto Daily Star* on October 11, 1909, due to the rarity of Chinese women, not only in Toronto, but across Canada. In 1921, Toronto had 2,019 Chinese males, 115 females.

Listen to Keith Lock talk about his grandmother and her publicized arrival in Toronto at www.tinyurl.com/rcwheadtax02.

### First Chinese Baby

Chinese women, like these ones pictured in Victoria, 1905, were rarely seen outdoors. They faced the same prejudice for being women regardless of whether they were in China or Canada. In 1861, Won Alexander Cumyow was the first Chinese person born in Canada.

### Women Rarely Seen

Chinese women comprised only 1 per cent of Canada's Chinese population in 1885. Their absence inhibited the growth of a second generation of Canadian-born Chinese. Another impact was the employment of Chinese men by white families as servants, cooks, and houseboys.

### Saved by the Church

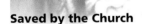

The Chinese Rescue Home in Victoria was established in 1888 by the Methodist Church for Chinese women and girls who had escaped a life of prostitution. There, they found a safe haven, a place where they studied English and Chinese for their conversion to Christianity. Similar homes opened in other towns in BC.

### Ahead of Her Time

In Canada, especially in the west, intermarriage was common between Chinese men and First Nations and other local women. Nellie Yip Quong, pictured here in 1908, was a Caucasian woman who stunned her family by marrying a successful Chinese jeweller, Charles Yip Quong, from Vancouver. A master of five Chinese dialects, she worked tirelessly as an advocate for her adopted community, providing health and social services denied to the Chinese, including delivering babies. She was designated a National Historic Person by the Canadian government in 2008.

Chinese Women in Canada

# CHALLENGING A HOSTILE COMMUNITY, 1900–1939

# Anti-Asian Violence

Non-white immigrants faced extraordinary challenges. The number of Japanese immigrants was restricted, blacks and Indians were discouraged from entering Canada. The Chinese were treated as racially inferior, and prejudice and discrimination prevented them from participation in Canadian life. They were relegated to the bottom of society with no economic or political influence. Racist attitudes forced the Chinese to stay together for mutual support and protection.

**Racist Vandalism**
In 1907, the Asiatic Exclusion League, formed to keep BC "white," incited an angry mob to march on the Chinese and Japanese stores in Vancouver. In Chinatown, buildings were vandalized and windows smashed. In the neighbouring Japantown, properties suffered less damage from the Vancouver Riot because the Japanese people there had time to board up their shops and fight off the mob.

REPORT

BY

W. L. MACKENZIE KING, C.M.G.
DEPUTY MINISTER OF LABOUR

COMMISSIONER

APPOINTED TO INVESTIGATE INTO THE

LOSSES SUSTAINED BY THE CHINESE POPULATION
OF VANCOUVER, B.C.

ON THE OCCASION OF THE RIOTS IN THAT CITY
IN SEPTEMBER, 1907

PRINTED BY ORDER OF PARLIAMENT

OTTAWA
PRINTED BY S. E. DAWSON, PRINTER TO THE KING'S MOST
EXCELLENT MAJESTY.
1908

[No. 74 /—1908.]

## Government Report

William Lyon Mackenzie King, deputy labour minister and future prime minister, investigated the claims for damages caused by the Vancouver Riot. His report recommended financial compensation for "the losses of Chinese residents in Vancouver, occasioned by anti-Asiatic riots." Chinese businesses received $26,000 in total. During King's investigation, he learned about the legal manufacture and sale of opium in BC. This discovery led to the creation of Canada's first anti-drug law.

# . . . losses sustained by the Chinese population of Vancouver . . .

## Racial Discrimination

Other hate-related violence occurred elsewhere. In 1913, a riot broke out in Nanaimo to protest the hiring of Chinese workers during a coal miners' strike. In 1919, Chinese cafés were looted in Halifax. In St. John's, Newfoundland, windows of Chinese laundries were smashed. Acts of racial discrimination were not limited to Chinese and Japanese people. In 1914, the ship, *Komagata Maru*, sailed into Vancouver with 375 Hindu, Indian, Sikh, and Muslim passengers who were refused permission to disembark. After two months of negotiations with immigration authorities, the navy escorted the ship from Canadian waters.

Anti-Asian Violence

# Legislated Racism and the Impact of the Head Tax

The $50 head tax did not achieve what had been intended because immigrants from China continued coming to Canada. The head tax was raised to $100 in 1900, then to $500 in 1903. It was a staggering amount, representing two years' pay for Chinese workers. In 1906, Newfoundland, still a British colony, levied a head tax of $300. Other countries, including the US, Australia, and New Zealand, also imposed head taxes for the same reason of discouraging Chinese immigration. Despite these heavy taxes, the Chinese were desperate to leave China and escape economic hardships. No matter the financial hurdles, they left in search of a chance to earn ten to twenty times more.

**No Vote Means No Professions**

In BC and Saskatchewan, the "Mongolian and Chinese race" was excluded from voting on the basis of race, despite efforts by labour organizations like the Co-operative Commonwealth Federation (now the New Democratic Party), which advocated equal treatment for Asian workers. Not being on the voters' lists had far-reaching implications in these two provinces. Not only were Chinese people excluded from nomination for political office, school trustees, and jury service, they were barred from professions like pharmacy, medicine, and law. K. Dock Yip, who was born in Vancouver, moved to Ontario where there were no such restrictions. He graduated from law school to become the first Chinese lawyer in Canada. Gretta Wong Grant, who was born in London, Ontario, was the first female Chinese-Canadian lawyer.

## LA TAXE DES CHINOIS

### IL LEUR EN COUTE MAINTENANT $500 AU LIEU DE $ POUR ENTRER DANS NOTRE PAYS.

Depuis que la nouvelle taxe imposable pour l'entrée des Chinois sur le sol canadien est mise en vigueur l'immigration a cessé. Cette taxe qui était autrefois de $50 est maintenant fixée à $500, ce qui demande chez les émigrants, une petite fortune qui pourrait les faire vivre relativement à l'aise dans ... quand le décompte est fait de la taxe, des frais de voyage, etc., on arrive à bien près de $1,000.

Lee Chu, le chef de la colonie chinoise à Montréal, questionné au sujet de la taxe nouvelle, nous a assuré que le droit d'entrée aurait pour effet de faire cesser l'émigration chinoise sur le Canada.

Lee Chu, nous a donné aussi la traduction du message envoyé en Chine, aux agences d'émigration. Ce message se lit comme suit :

A nos frères de Chine,

Vous êtes par les présentes avertis que vous aurez à payer $500 pour entrer sur le sol canadien.

LEE CHU.

自西人正月一号趑定
我華人税金銀伍佰
尤元請為秋一大也
李仲筆啟

**News Report**

A Montreal news article reports on the increase of the head tax to $500. To pay for it, Chinese immigrants borrowed money from their friends, relatives, and fellow villagers to come to Canada. Years of hard work would pass before they were able to repay these loans.

Vancouver Crystal Pool, Corner Beach Avenue and Nicola St., Vancouver, British Columbia

WHITE IMMIGRATION / ORIENTAL EXCLUSION

B.C. IMMIGRATION POLICY

### Segregation and Bans

On a daily basis, the Chinese faced discrimination. They were banned from swimming in the Vancouver Crystal Pool. One store prohibited Chinese customers from shopping on Saturdays from 7 to 10 p.m. In Victoria, the Chinese could sit only in the upper level of the Opera House. One restaurant had a racist sign: "No Indians, Chinese, or dogs allowed."

### Anti-Chinese Cartoon

Anti-Chinese racism was regularly depicted in newspapers and magazines. This 1907 political cartoon shows the exclusion of "Orientals" behind a locked gate in contrast to the welcoming of white immigrants through an open gate.

### First Female Doctor

Victoria Cheung graduated from the University of Toronto as the first female Chinese doctor in Canada. Like K. Dock Yip, she was born in BC and had to move to Ontario to study for her chosen profession. With a university scholarship from the Women's Missionary Society, she graduated and fulfilled her dream of being a medical missionary in China.

### No White Female Workers

Saskatchewan, Manitoba, and Ontario prohibited Chinese employers from hiring white females in laundries for fear that the women would be corrupted. In some cities, including Lethbridge, Vancouver, and Hamilton, the Chinese could not open laundries in white, middle-class neighbourhoods. In 1894, William P. Hubbard, Toronto's first black politician, was among the few elected officials who stood up for Chinese laundry owners.

Legislated Racism and the Impact of the Head Tax

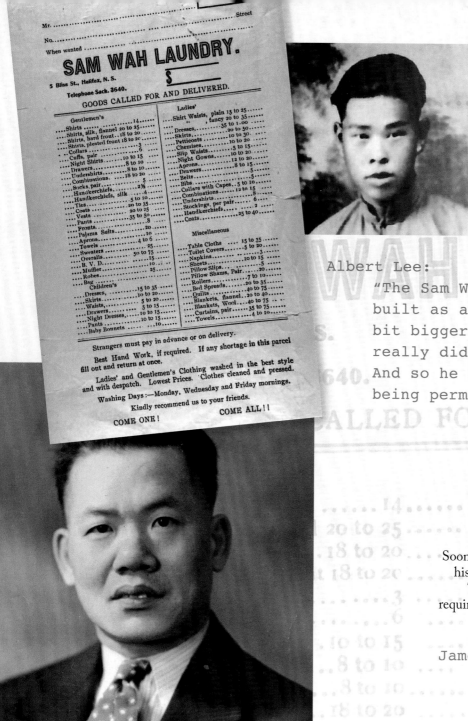

SAM WAH LAUNDRY.
5 Bliss St., Halifax, N. S.
Telephone Sack. 3640.
GOODS CALLED FOR AND DELIVERED.

## Long Trip

Albert Lee's grandfather, Ngoon Lee, arrived in Canada and paid the $500 head tax in 1906. He travelled to Halifax because of his connection with the Fongs who had lived in the neighbouring village in China. The Fongs were the first Chinese people to settle in Halifax. Ngoon Lee opened Sam Wah Laundry. Ten years later, he paid the $500 head tax to bring over his nine-year-old son, the first Chinese boy to live in Halifax and the future father of Albert.

Albert Lee:
"The Sam Wah Laundry was originally built as a boat shed. It was a little bit bigger than a two-car garage. He really didn't quite feel welcome here. And so he had mixed feelings about being permanently here."

## Hardships for Son

Soon Long Pon paid the head taxes for his wife and five-year-old son, James. The family suffered financially and required twelve-year-old James to move away from his family to work.

James Pon:
"I had to pay the head tax, which was $500 and my mother had to pay the $500 head tax, a total of $1,000, which was quite a sum of money in those days. It was 1922 and it took my father 17 years to repay this $1,000 loan."

## First Job in Canada

Sid Chow Tan's grandfather, Norman Chow Gim Tan, paid the $500 head tax at the age of nineteen. His first job was shovelling coal.

Sid Chow Tan:
"They shoved the coal down a hole, which would go directly into the basement. That was his first job and he slept down there too. He said it was worse than being a dog."

Chapter 3: Challenging a Hostile Community, 1900–1939

Walter Tom:

"Each homecoming would have been welcomed by so many appreciative relatives who relied on the money that was sent by my grandfather from Canada. Here's an uncle, here's a cousin. It seemed that the whole village was related to us one way or the other."

**Financial Burden**

Charlie Quan, holding his head tax certificate, came to Canada in 1923 as a sixteen-year-old. "My uncle lent me the $500. We had so much hardship. It was hard to make a living in China."

Judi Michelle Young:

"We have no idea where he acquired the funds [for the head tax]. He probably borrowed, like everyone else."

**LISTEN TO THE AUDIO**

**Head Tax Times Three**

Judi Michelle Young's father, Yong Hong Yan, paid the head tax three times after returning to Canada from his visits to China. During these trips, he married three times. He outlived his first two wives and married his third wife in the 1930s. By that time, he was in his seventies.

🔊 Listen to Judi Michelle Young describe the impact of the head tax on her father at www.tinyurl.com/rcwheadtax14.

**Elderly Groom**

Hong Tai Wong married his first wife in China at a young age after paying her $500 head tax. Later widowed, he married Germaine Wong's mother-to-be when he was sixty-five years old.

Germaine Wong:

"In China, people were dying of hunger. If the men stayed in the villages, their lot would not have improved. America was one of the few options."

# Chinese Life, 1900–1914

The Chinese settled in Chinatowns for safety from discrimination. Racial prejudice had the impact of forcing the Chinese to stay together, thereby strengthening Chinatowns. By the early 1900s, Chinese communities in BC were thriving. Vancouver, now with the largest Chinese population and Chinatown in Canada, surpassed Victoria in size. Across the country, over 90 per cent of Chinese people lived in or near their Chinatowns, in cities like Calgary, Moose Jaw, Winnipeg, Toronto, and Hamilton. Most Chinese in the province of Quebec settled in Montreal and the community there soon rivalled the one in Toronto. Like Edmonton and Saskatoon, Quebec City was not on the railway route so its Chinese population grew more slowly. The Atlantic provinces, on the other hand, had sparse Chinese settlement.

**Work Without Fear**
Hop Wah Laundry in St. John's was one of twenty Chinese laundries in Newfoundland and Labrador in the early 1930s. Cleaning clothes was considered women's work but the Chinese established themselves in this business. With little start-up money, they could work, eat, and live in their laundries without fear of discrimination from white employers.

Chapter 3: Challenging a Hostile Community, 1900–1939

## Bachelor Societies

Typically, Chinese communities were made up of single men in what came to be known as bachelor societies. It was unusual among the Chinese to have a family in Canada because the head tax made it financially prohibitive to bring wives, children, and parents. Eighty per cent of the men had left wives behind in China. Bachelor-society men saved money in as many ways as possible, like living in rundown, crowded rooming houses. Their frugal lifestyles allowed them to send regular remittances to their families in China. The more successful men made occasional trips to China — unmarried men to get married, married ones to visit their wives and father children.

# It was unusual among the Chinese to have a family in Canada because the head tax made it financially prohibitive to bring wives, children, and parents.

## Republic of China

In large part due to the fundraising efforts of Dr. Sun Yat-sen in Canada and around the world, the Manchu government was overthrown in 1911 and the Republic of China established the following year. A political cartoon shows a Chinese soldier cutting off a man's queue, which had been forced upon Chinese men by the Manchus. Up until this time, many had been reluctant to cut them off. In the event that they had returned to live in China, they would have been required by law to have this hairstyle.

Chinese Life, 1900-1914

# Canada in the First World War

The Great War, or the First World War, was set in motion when the heir to the Austro-Hungarian Empire was assassinated by a Serbian in 1914. On one side of the battlefield was Austria-Hungary, on the opposite side, Serbia, Russia, France, and Britain. Of course, Canada was at war too as a member of the British Commonwealth. Although many Chinese tried to enlist in the Canadian Army, they were refused by recruiters in BC on the grounds that this was a "white man's war." Despite the racial discrimination of the head tax and other anti-Chinese legislation, an estimated 300 Chinese men, Canadian-born and naturalized, volunteered to serve in the army. Many left BC to enlist in other provinces, like Ontario, where there were no restrictions.

RECRUITS WANTED

Apply
91ST.
HIGHLANDERS
ORDERLY ROOM
Armouries, Hamilton
PAY BEGINS
AT ONCE

**Cheated of the Franchise**
The Chinese war veterans who served in the army proved their loyalty to Canada. Although they were granted the right to vote due to their war service, they never got to take advantage of the franchise. The *Dominion Elections Act*, enacted in 1920, did not allow any Chinese person to vote, regardless of the promise that had been made to the veterans.

They were refused by recruiters in BC on the grounds that this was a "white man's war."

**CANADIAN PACIFIC RAILWAY**

## Private Instructions to Guards in Charge of Chinese

### Labourers Needed

A labour shortage prompted Britain to ask its ally, China, to provide 200,000 labourers for war construction projects in France. Canada agreed to transport 80,000 of them. Guards, who followed the instruction manual shown above, kept watch on the train. The fear was that the Chinese would escape onto Canadian soil without paying the head tax.

### En Route to the Front

The *Empress of Russia* transported the first of many shiploads of labourers from China. After landing in BC, they travelled cross-country to Halifax in sealed railway cars, then back on ships to cross the Atlantic Ocean to the western front in France. There, they loaded and unloaded supplies from ships and trains, filled sandbags, built roads and railways, and dug trenches.

### Tell No One

The Chinese Labour Corps, as the workers became known, were outfitted with straw hats and dark blue tunics and pants. They are seen disembarking from a ship for quarantine at William Head, BC.
As late as 1919, the Chinese labourers helped bury the dead and clean up the battlefields. Afterwards, they were shipped back to China. The Canadian government enforced a media blackout about these workers and their contribution remained top secret for many years.

### No Rest

When there was a stopover in Ontario, the Chinese labourers were put to work at Camp Petawawa, a Canadian Forces base and internment camp for German, Austrian, and Italian prisoners of war. The Chinese Labour Corps was the largest ethnic minority group to participate in the Great War.

# The Exclusion *Act*

The successive head taxes of $50, $100, and $500 failed to curb Chinese immigration. On July 1, 1923, the federal government enacted the *Chinese Immigration Act*, known in the Chinese communities as the "Chinese Exclusion Act." This was the most comprehensive law to exclude the Chinese from entering Canada. With the exception of merchants, students, and diplomats, all Chinese people were denied entry for the sole reason of their race. Trips to China were limited to a maximum of two years' absence; otherwise, entry back into Canada would be denied.

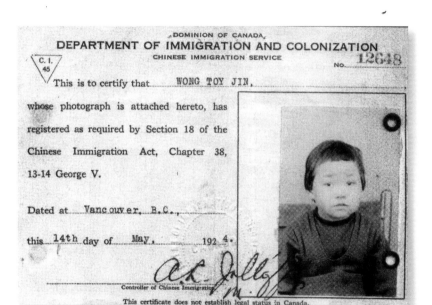

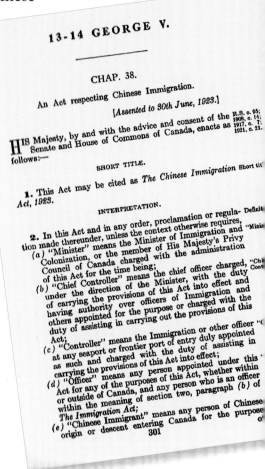

**Identification Papers**

The *Chinese Immigration Act* also stipulated that every Chinese person, whether or not they were born in Canada, was required to register for an identification card. This one for Toy Jin Wong (Jean Lumb) was issued when she was four years old. Jean would later help to change Canada's immigration laws and become the first Chinese-Canadian woman to receive the Order of Canada, the country's highest civilian honour.

**Hard Labour**

These women, working on road construction in Kowloon, China, show the hardship faced by the wives who were left behind during the Chinese exclusionary period. While some men could afford a trip or two to China to visit their families and father children, many women endured a lifetime of spousal separation.

**Humiliation Day**

As the *Chinese Immigration Act* was being drafted, many individuals, missionaries, and organizations, including a committee of eight representatives from the Chinese community that travelled to Ottawa, voiced their objections. Their efforts were unsuccessful and the *Chinese Immigration Act* became law on July 1. While Canadians celebrated Dominion Day, the Chinese in Canada boycotted any public holiday festivities on the day referred to by the Chinese as Humiliation Day. Their businesses were closed and Canadian flags were not displayed.

Chapter 3: Challenging a Hostile Community, 1900–1939

Sid Chow Tan:

"[My grandfather] told his father not to
sell his sister, that he would go to work.
He was seven, she was ten. As it turned
out, his father did not sell the sister. My
grandfather sent money back to his sister
[in China] all his life."

### Young Married Couple

Albert Lee's father, Chuck Lee, returned
to China at age eighteen to get married
in 1926. By tradition, the marriage was
arranged by a matchmaker so he did not
meet his teenaged bride, Sui Fa Kung, until
the wedding day. He returned to Canada; she
stayed behind in China.

Albert Lee:

"Head tax is money
paid and that is one
thing for people who
paid and worked it
off. The *Exclusion Act*
was a whole different
matter, which was for
fifteen years they
were separated."

### Sons Preferred

The birth of three sons would have
been celebrated in any Chinese family
due to the preference for male children.
Germaine Wong was told of her father's
disappointment when she was born instead
of a son. Her arrival was also considered
extremely unlucky because she was a girl
child born in the Year of the Tiger.

### Remittances

The Chinese sent money to China to feed
their families and buy land. Homes, like this
one in Kaiping, could be sturdily build for
protection from flooding and bandits. Money
from overseas Chinese was also used to build
roads, schools, and hospitals in their villages.

Walter Tom:

"The overseas Chinese
followed very closely
with what was
happening at home.
The money that they
sent back was the
lifeline to their
families in China."

The Exclusion Act

# The Fight for Survival in the Interwar Period

Life for the Chinese in the years between the wars was the saddest of times. They faced the challenges of a bachelor life with no families, long hours working at their jobs and businesses, and the Great Depression — all under a cloud of uncertainty. The Communist Party of China and the Nationalist Party (Guomindang) divided allegiances as they struggled against each other to seize control in China. Even worse, China faced its greatest enemy — Japan. The Sino-Japanese War erupted in 1937 and the Japanese occupied China. Little news filtered through so there were worries about the safety of families left to fend for themselves without husbands and sons.

**Bachelor-Society Men**

After the Chinese moved east from BC to other provinces, they opened laundries, restaurants, and grocery stores along the railway route. These laundry employees were among the one hundred bachelor-society men in Brockville, Ontario, where there were only two families. In Halifax, Sam Wah Laundry was the gathering place where the bachelor men congregated. "There would be half a dozen or ten men, who were married with wives in China. They would go there to socialize and probably have familiar village food," remembers Albert Lee. By 1941, over 20,000 Chinese families lived apart, with husbands in Canada, and wives and children in China.

**Farming**

Farming was familiar for the Chinese, who had emigrated from a country where 80 per cent of the people were farmers. In BC, fruits and vegetables were grown on farms and delivered to homes, stores, and restaurants. Chinese farm workers earned $20 to $25 a month in 1900, while white workers made $30 to $40. Typically, the Chinese performing the same jobs earned about half the wage of white workers.

**Survival**
Gim Wong, pictured above, lived with his family at the back of a laundry. The roof leaked; the floor was cement. The toilet was outside in the woodshed.

Albert Wong:

"[My father] had to go pick blueberries . . . There weren't many other prospects back then, other forms of work."

**Good Food, Cheap Prices**
After laundries, restaurants and cafés were the second most popular Chinese business. The ones located in the downtown areas were busy with office workers, sales clerks, and shoppers. Tasty and reasonably priced meals of Western food attracted customers. Chinese restaurants, always open seven days a week, slowly introduced Chinese dishes adapted for Western tastes.

James Pon:

"I would get up at the crack of dawn to work in my father's restaurant, then go to school, and work in the restaurant until midnight. All four of us brothers and sisters completed university working under the same conditions."

**Don't Call Us**
Albert Lee's father, Chuck Lee (seated in front row), was the only Asian student at Le Marchant Street School in Halifax. Although he graduated as the first Chinese civil engineer from the Nova Scotia Technical College, racial prejudice allowed him to practise his profession for only a few years.

Albert Lee:

"When he applied for different jobs, they basically would tell him that the job was already taken or 'don't call us, we'll call you.'"

The Fight for Survival in the Interwar Period

## Sense of Belonging

Chinese parents considered the Boy Scouts a good way to integrate their sons into Canadian society. In the 1930s, nearly all of Toronto's Chinese-Canadian boys were in the 128th Scout Troop.

## Sports as Equalizers

Chinese sports teams showed that they were just as good or better when playing by the same rules. The Chinese Students Soccer Team of Vancouver was inducted into the BC Sports Hall of Fame, along with soccer player Quene Yip.

## Whites Before Chinese

Anti-Chinese discrimination did not diminish during the Great Depression. The Canadian government offered one-way tickets to China to avoid the cost of social assistance for the Chinese. It also lengthened the time that the Chinese could travel outside of Canada from two to four years as a measure to save on government aid, even though the Chinese received $1.12, half of what was paid to non-Chinese applicants. In Calgary, a city politician insisted that "white people should be looked after before Chinese."

Chapter 3: Challenging a Hostile Community, 1900–1939

## Unfair Treatment

During the Depression years, a third of Canadian workers were unemployed and one in five relied on government aid. Long lineups at soup kitchens were commonplace. The Chinese first turned to their associations, which supported them as long as possible. By 1931, 80 per cent of Chinatown residents in Vancouver were jobless. When 145 Chinese died of malnutrition, there were angry protests about their 16-cent meal tickets while others received ones worth 25 cents.

## No News

Chinese newspapers were eagerly read for news from China but they lacked information about loved ones. Money could no longer be sent back home due to war disruptions. Judi Michelle Young's father did not know about his infant son's death and his wife's expulsion from her home.

Walter Tom:

"The hardest time was during the war. The families were suffering. My grandmother died because of the conditions during that time. There was nothing to eat."

## Who Is This Woman?

Madame Chiang Kai-shek, the wife of China's military and political leader, visited Canada to raise relief funds for the Chinese war effort against Japan. Because she was educated in the US, her charm and command of the English language helped to change the North American perception of the Chinese people.

## Anything To Help China

With so much instability in China, the Chinese in Canada raised money to buy airplanes, medical supplies, food for the war orphans, and munitions to fight Japan's occupation. Parades, church bazaars, music and opera performances, and other community events were organized for fundraising.

The Fight for Survival in the Interwar Period

# CANADA AT WAR, 1939–1945

# Canada Enters the Second World War

In 1939, France, Britain, Canada, and other Commonwealth countries were plunged into the Second World War by Germany. By 1940, Canada was forced to conscript eligible Canadians who were ordered by law to join the army. In BC and Saskatchewan, the Chinese were excluded from conscription as "unwanted soldiers." This did not stop many Chinese Canadians from volunteering for service.

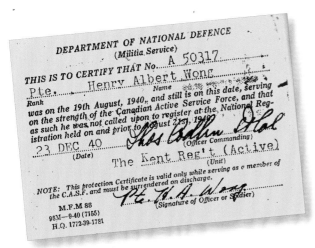

DEPARTMENT OF NATIONAL DEFENCE
(Militia Service)

THIS IS TO CERTIFY THAT No. A 50317

Pte. Henry Albert Wong
Rank                    Name
was on the 19th August, 1940, and still is on this date, serving on the strength of the Canadian Active Service Force, and that as such he was not called upon to register at the National Registration held on and prior to August 21st, 1940.

23 DEC 40                    Thos Bodkin DtoL
(Date)                    (Officer Commanding)

The Kent Reg't (Active)
(Unit)

NOTE: This protection Certificate is valid only while serving as a member of the C.A.S.F. and must be surrendered on discharge.

M.F.M 88                    Pte H. A. Wong
96M—9-40 (7155)            (Signature of Officer or Soldier)
H.Q. 1772-39-1781

### To Fight or Not to Fight

The Chinese in Canada were divided about their participation in the war. Some were bitter about the anti-Chinese laws, including the denial of the vote. Others, like Douglas Jung, wanted "to show to the Canadian people, and to the Canadian government, that we were willing to work for everything that we wanted, which was no more than the rights of Canadian privileges, the rights that every other Canadian enjoys."

### Air Force and Navy Say No

The Royal Canadian Air Force and Royal Canadian Navy refused Chinese enlisters until 1942. Instead, Hank Wong volunteered with the army in 1940.

Hank Wong:

```
"You can't go in the
navy. They're not
allowed to bring Chinese
. . . . You must be of
white race."
```

**The Mosquito**
Canada's aviation industry boomed during the Second World War. It produced over 16,000 military aircraft, including the de Havilland Mosquito, which served as a bomber and fighter plane.

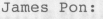

**Award-Winning Design**
James Pon (r) worked as a design engineer at de Havilland Aircraft Company. He received a Governor General's Medal for the design of a riveting gun that helped increase the wartime production of the Mosquito.

**From Gunner to Engineer**
Gim Wong was a twenty-two-year-old when he enlisted in the air force. Although he trained as an air gunner, he became a flight engineer and the youngest commissioned officer from the Chinese community. His three brothers also served during the war.

James Pon:

"[In] a space marked 'Race' I wrote down 'Oriental.' The employment officer erased it and wrote in 'Caucasian.' If he hadn't changed [it], I could not have been hired."

**Call for Service**
The war effort needed more manpower. Although Chinese Canadians were excluded from conscription in 1940, they were finally called into service in 1944. They fought shoulder-to-shoulder with their fellow Canadians.

Canada Enters the Second World War

**Everyone Pitches In**

Chinese-Canadian women, like these ones in Toronto, helped raise money for the war effort by doing fund drives, knitting sweaters, socks, and mitts for the soldiers, and collecting pots and pans to melt down to make guns and ammunition. Children pitched in by collecting paper, metal, and other items for recycling.

**Six Hundred Chinese Canadians**

L. Mar was the only Chinese Canadian in the Parachute Battalion. Six hundred Chinese Canadians served in all three branches of the armed forces to serve alongside their fellow Canadians on land, sea, and air.

# Six hundred Chinese Canadians served in all three branches of the armed forces . . .

**Women in Trades**

Up until the war, Chinese women in Canada had been limited by cultural tradition to a small circle of family and friends. Now, they enlisted in the armed forces, volunteered as air-raid wardens and first-aid workers, and worked in wartime industries in historically male-dominated trades, like welding and engine repair. After the war, women became more active in their communities.

Chapter 4: Canada at War, 1939–1945

**Raising Money**

Chinese communities across Canada held parades, like this one in Vancouver, to help promote the sale of Victory Bonds and other fundraising events. For the first time, they had a chance to work side by side with other Canadians for aid agencies like the Red Cross.

**Victory Bonds**

The Chinese community wholeheartedly responded to the Canadian government's campaign to buy Victory Bonds and purchased $10 million worth to support Canadian soldiers and the war effort.

Albert Lee:

"There was a lot of suffering and uncertainty for our mother and our sister living in China at the time."

**Cut Off**

Wing Nun Eng couldn't send money to his wife, Fung Hi Tom, in China. Newfoundland was virtually locked down because it was a vital geographic location to defend Canada against German submarines.

Walter Tom:

"Most families were more concerned about how their families were doing overseas. That was their big concern."

# China and Canada Become Allies

After the bombing of Pearl Harbor on December 7, 1941, the US declared war on Japan. By evening, Canada also declared war. For the first time, Japan was the common enemy of both China and Canada. This turn of events had a dramatic impact on Canadians, who gained more sympathy for the Chinese, their homeland, and their war effort against Japan. Sid Chow Tan remembers his grandfather saying, "It was such a great thing that China was an ally. Of course, during the war, we were fighting the same enemy."

### Japanese Internment
In 1942, the Canadian government relocated 21,000 Japanese people in BC to internment camps, even though over 75 per cent were Canadian citizens. Many Chinese pinned handmade badges stating "I'm Chinese" on their clothing so they would not be mistaken for Japanese.

### Operation Oblivion
When the British government needed Chinese-Canadian recruits in 1944, being Chinese was suddenly an asset, not a liability. A secret mission, under the code name Operation Oblivion, was planned to sabotage, demolish, infiltrate, and spy behind enemy lines in Southeast Asia. Over 100 Chinese Canadians volunteered despite the slim chance of survival in this operation.

Douglas Jung:
> "Unless we volunteered to serve Canada during this hour of need, we would be in a very difficult position after the war ended to demand our rights as Canadian citizens."

Listen to Douglas Jung describe his experience at www.tinyurl.com/rcwheadtax00

**LISTEN TO THE AUDIO**

## Pearl Harbor

The *USS Arizona*, now memorialized as an American National Historic Landmark, was one of the battleships that was attacked in Pearl Harbor. Less than eight hours afterwards, Japan invaded Hong Kong, which was valiantly but unsuccessfully defended by two Canadian battalions, the Royal Rifles of Canada and the Winnipeg Grenadiers.

## End of the War

After six years of devastation and the loss of nine million lives, the Second World War ended in Europe on May 8, 1945, and three months later in the Pacific on August 15. Japan, the country that had invaded and occupied China and Hong Kong, was defeated. This victorious day was especially celebrated in Chinese communities across Canada, such as in Halifax.

**LISTEN TO THE AUDIO**

### Top Secret

The story of Operation Oblivion remained a secret for twenty-five year under Canada's *Official Secrets Act*. Hank Wong, the last surviving Oblivion member, received a letter of appreciation from the government in 1988 for his bravery.

🔊 Listen to Hank Wong talk about Operation Oblivion at www.tinyurl.com/rcwheadtax05.

On behalf of the Government of Canada, I wish to extend my warmest congratulations to a very special group of veterans.

Not only did this gallant band of Chinese Canadians volunteer for wartime service, they did so knowing that they would be signing up for some extremely dangerous and hazardous missions.

That was courage and commitment beyond the call of duty. Canada was fortunate to have such selfless men.

The list names on the plaque being unveiled today is truly a roll call of honour. Their contribution in war inspired overdue recognition for every Chinese Canadian in peacetime. Such a legacy will never lose its value.

OTTAWA
1988

**Hank Wong:**

"The Americans had all the troops, all the machines, all the air, all the airplanes, and all the vessels to take their boys home. How are you going to get the Canadians home?"

### War Bride

Joan Lim On, a war bride who married Sergeant Tom Lock in Australia, wasn't allowed entry into Canada due to the *Chinese Immigration Act*. Tom wasn't allowed to live in Australia because of that country's Exclusion Act. Eventually, she was granted special permission to come to Canada.

**Keith Lock:**

"As [my mother] was leaving, the Australian official said to her, 'You're welcome to come back to Australia any time, as an Australian citizen, but don't bring your husband.'"

🔊 Listen to Keith Lock talk about his parents' dilemma at www.tinyurl.com/rcwheadtax06.

China and Canada Become Allies

# CHAPTER 5

# CHALLENGES AND CHANGES, 1945–1990

# Fighting for Rights

The end of the war marked a turning point in changing attitudes about the Chinese in Canada. Chinese-Canadian men and women had served alongside other Canadians despite earlier barriers over their enlistment. Chinese communities raised millions of dollars for the war effort. China was an ally. The Holocaust and Germany's shameful treatment of minorities forced Canada and other countries to reassess their own racist policies. The US repealed its Chinese exclusionary legislation. Finally, the Universal Declaration of Human Rights by the United Nations heralded a new era of liberty, equality, and freedom. Canada repealed the *Chinese Immigration Act* in 1947 and voting rights were extended to the Chinese.

**Top-Secret Mission**
General George R. Pearkes was one of only two Canadian officers who knew about Operation Oblivion. As Douglas Jung described, "We were so secret in our operations . . . the military refused to recognize that we had been overseas. We had to contact General Pearkes to confirm that we had been overseas."

# Canada repealed the *Chinese Immigration Act* in 1947.

## CERTIFICATE OF CANADIAN CITIZENSHIP

**Becoming a Citizen**

The *Citizenship Act* granted Canadian citizenship to all British subjects born or naturalized in Canada. Immigrants could apply for citizenship if they met the requirements, including Canadian residency and adequate knowledge of French or English. Germaine Wong's mother had difficulties in passing the test to obtain her Canadian citizenship.

Germaine Wong:

"She couldn't speak English or French. She didn't have a clue what the questions were asking. Two questions really stumped her [about two official languages and the two railways]. She finally got it but it was so horrific an experience."

**The Franchise**

The Chinese gained the right to vote all across Canada in 1947. Won Alexander Cumyow, the first Chinese person born in Canada, voted for the first time in 1949 at the age of 88.

Sid Chow Tan:

"I've never missed a vote in my life. My grandfather didn't either. We would go together. We're talking about every vote. My grandmother as well."

**A Political Voice**
Now that Chinese Canadians could vote, they were allowed to become professionals, like lawyers and doctors, and run for public office. Douglas Jung, a war veteran, became a lawyer and the first Chinese-Canadian Member of Parliament (MP).

a man of *thought* *
a man of *action* *
a man of *achievement* *

**DOUG JUNG** *
**Centre's Conservative Candidate**

> # Douglas Jung, a war veteran, became a lawyer and the first Chinese-Canadian Member of Parliament.

**Another First**
Douglas Jung was appointed the first Chinese-Canadian delegate at the United Nations. A nineteen-storey federal building in Vancouver is named to commemorate him.

**Persistence Pays Off**

After raising her children, James Pon's wife, Vera, wanted to study computer programming. She was discouraged from applying because the college registrar said that a Chinese woman wouldn't be able to find a job.

Vera Pon:

> "The drop-out rate was very high. However, me being a persistent-type person and hard worker, I graduated with honours at the top of the class and three job offers."

# Although she was Canadian-born, she lost her citizenship . . . and became "alien," the status of her . . . husband.

**Citizenship Restored**

Married women, like Jean Lumb, took on the status of their husbands. Although she was Canadian-born, she lost her citizenship in 1939 and became "alien," the status of her Chinese-born husband. She applied for citizenship twenty years later and became a citizenship court judge who presided over ceremonies and administered the oath of citizenship to over 1,000 Canadians.

# Family Reunification and Paper Sons and Daughters

With the repeal of the *Chinese Immigration Act* in 1947, there should have been a joyous reunification of families. While Europeans flooded into Canada, there remained strict requirements, including age and citizenship, for the Chinese to sponsor their families. A scheme for buying false identity papers became widespread as a way to bring children over as "paper sons and daughters." For example, an eighteen-year-old son who exceeded the age limit would enter Canada with the identification papers of a younger boy and become another family's son.

**Stranger in the Family**
Wives and children faced challenges of adapting to a new country and living with husbands and fathers who were often strangers to them. Judi Michelle Young's mother was widowed shortly after her arrival.

Judi Michelle Young:
"She had to support the family. She was totally illiterate, spoke ... no English. She didn't make much money when being paid sixty-five cents for [sewing] a dozen blouses."

**LISTEN TO THE AUDIO**

**Three Sons**
Shortly after Albert Lee's mother and sister arrived in Halifax, his mother bore three sons in rapid succession. She was in her late thirties and early forties. His father was old enough to be his grandfather. Albert, pictured with his brothers, imitates children who made fun of his Chinese eyes.

Albert Lee:
"Our sister, Nancy, was fifteen years old and had never seen her father except in photographs."

Listen to Albert Lee talk about his mother and sister's arrival in Halifax at www.tinyurl.com/rcwheadtax11.

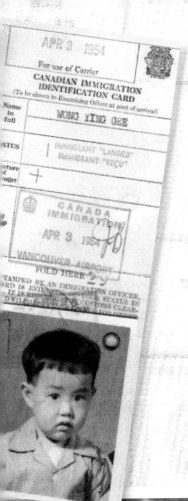

### Life in Montreal

Germaine Wong arrived in Montreal as a four-year-old with her mother. The family lived in a rooming house in Chinatown and her mother worked with her father in the laundry.

Germaine Wong:
"My father was quite ill by the time we arrived. She single-handedly raised me, took care of my brother's family in China, and my father, and then the laundry . . . A lot of Chinese women were in that same situation. They arrived here not speaking the language, being in a culturally different place."

### Life in Newfoundland

Fung Hi Tom (l) left China to join her husband in Newfoundland, where she cooked at his restaurant, Rose Gardens. Hamburgers, fish and chips, and sandwiches were served along with Chinese sweet and sour dishes.

Fung Hi Tom:
"I didn't know how to make chicken balls . . . A friend who owned a restaurant taught me."

### Life in Saskatchewan

Coming from the only Chinese family in Battleford, Sid Chow Tan faced name-calling on a regular basis. "People would use the word 'chink' around us as if we weren't there."

Judi Michelle Young:
"He did talk about how the local white folks, adults and children, would throw rocks at them on a daily basis while they worked."

### Paper Son

Sid Chow Tan, who came to Saskatchewan as a one-year-old, was the paper son of his grandparents. His parents remained in China, separated from their son until their arrival twenty-two years later.

Sid Chow Tan:
"China-born and Canadian-made, that's me. I arrived as an illegal immigrant. I lived in fear of being deported."

▶️ Watch Sid Chow Tan talk about paper sons at http://tinyurl.com/rcwheadtax13

### Asking for Changes

For twenty years, a delegation went to Ottawa to ask for immigration changes to ease family reunification. Sitting next to Prime Minister John Diefenbaker is Wong Foon Sien, later designated a National Historic Person, and Jean Lumb. By 1971, only 1,558 families lived apart, a successful outcome of the delegation visits.

Family Reunification and Paper Sons and Daughters

# Changing Attitudes

Starting in 1960, the Chinese Adjustment Program allowed paper sons and daughters to apply for legal status. More significantly, Canada's immigration policy was overhauled in 1967. For the first time since 1885, the Chinese applied for entry on equal footing with other immigrants. Waves of newcomers arrived, first from Hong Kong, then from Vietnam, Taiwan, and China, bringing with them a diversity of skills, languages, and traditions.

**Bachelor Societies End**
The bachelor societies of men ended as families were reunited after years of separation. Today, family life flourishes not only in Chinatown but in residential areas with other Canadians. Intermarriage, which had not been socially acceptable, also has become commonplace, especially among the younger generations.

**Participation as Canadians**
Chinese Canadians have embraced the Canadian way of life and participated in mainstream community events outside of Chinatown, like the Calgary Stampede parade. In 1958, Jenny Chow was the first Chinese Canadian crowned as Miss Calgary Stampede.

## Multiculturalism
Under the leadership of Prime Minister Pierre Elliott Trudeau in 1971, Canada was the first country in the world to introduce a groundbreaking policy on multiculturalism. It recognizes all Canadians as full and equal participants in Canadian society and protects ethnic, racial, linguistic, and religious diversity.

## A Diverse Canada
The *Canadian Multiculturalism Act* was enacted as law in 1988. The *Canadian Charter of Rights and Freedoms* and the *Bill of Rights* are other important laws that instill tolerance and respect for all groups, making Canada a desirable destination for immigrants. Chinese Canadians who had been relegated to the bottom rung of society as working-class people began to build a middle class.

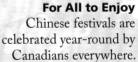

## For All to Enjoy
Chinese festivals are celebrated year-round by Canadians everywhere.

## Chinatowns Become Mainstream
In the early years, the Chinese were segregated from mainstream society and Chinatown was considered as a place that was off limits for respectable people. Now, Chinatowns across Canada are popular destinations for everyone.

**THE ASIANADIAN**

AN ASIAN CANADIAN MAGAZINE          THE ASIANADIAN VOL. 6 NO. 2

### Chinese-Canadian Media

*The Asianadian* covered cultural, political, and social issues for the Asian-Canadian community from 1978 to 1985. It was the first magazine to publish the works of now well-known Canadian writers including Paul Yee, Sky Lee, and Joy Kogawa. Today, there are many newspapers, magazines, and television and radio stations reporting on current events in Chinese and English.

### First Magazine

Chinese Canadians needed a voice to express their opinions. *Chinatown News* (1953–1996), founded by war veteran Roy Mah, was the most influential English-language magazine on the life of the Chinese in Canada and a vehicle to champion changes to the immigration laws after the repeal of the *Chinese Immigration Act.*

**Chinatown News**

Volume 30/Number 1/September 3/1982 • 60 cents

### Not to Be Ignored

A new age of activism emerged with the influx of well-educated and politically savvy immigrants from Hong Kong. Many issues have mobilized nationwide protests.

A new age of activism emerged with the influx of well-educated and politically savvy immigrants from Hong Kong.

### Fight for Equality

When "Campus Giveaway" was aired on CTV's current events program *W5* on September 30, 1979, Chinese Canadians rallied across the country to protest the racist contents of its televised report. Incorrect and misleading information suggested that international students were over-represented at Canadian universities, to the detriment of Canadian students. Canadian-born students of Chinese heritage were labelled as foreigners. The anti-*W5* campaign was successful in obtaining a public apology from CTV, a historic milestone in the rights of the Chinese in Canada.

### Organizing Across Canada

The anti-*W5* protest movement launched the formation of the Chinese Canadian National Council for Equality, now the Chinese Canadian National Council, at this press conference in 1979. This national organization has many branches across the country and continues its vigilance in defending the rights of Chinese Canadians.

### Tiananmen Square Protest

In 1989, millions of citizens filled Tiananmen Square in Beijing to protest the Chinese government and to demand democratic reform. Rallies in Canadian cities, like this one in Montreal, showed their solidarity against China's military response that left hundreds of civilians killed or injured.

### On the Watch

Chinese Canadians remain vigilant in safeguarding their hard-won rights for equality. In 2010, for instance, *Maclean's* magazine published an article about Canadian universities being "too Asian." Although the article was deemed racist and condemned by many universities and community organizations, and numerous municipal governments passed motions, the magazine did not make an apology.

Changing Attitudes

# CHAPTER 6
# ACKNOWLEDGING THE PAST, 1990–2006

# The Fight for Redress

From 1885 to 1923, 81,000 Chinese immigrants paid a total of $23 million in head taxes. The *Chinese Immigration Act* then stopped virtually all Chinese immigration for the next twenty-three years. The most devastating impact was the bachelor societies of men living without their wives and children. Although the Canadian government in 1980 passed a motion recognizing "the contribution made to the Canadian mosaic and culture by the people of Chinese background," this was not enough.

### Gathering Support

A national campaign was ignited to seek a formal response from the government for the head tax and the *Chinese Immigration Act*. Some people wanted an apology while others wanted financial compensation or both. Over 4,000 head tax payers, their spouses, and their descendants registered with the Chinese Canadian National Council and its partners, like the BC Coalition of Head Tax Payers, Spouses, and Descendants, to lobby the federal government on their behalf.

### One Man's Quest

Sid Chow Tan got involved with the head tax redress movement from day one. "It's about the justice. I just want to tell our story so that my grandfather and my grandmother can get the justice and honour they deserve."

▶ Watch Sid Chow Tan talk about the impact of the head tax on his family at www.youtube.com/watch?v=k9EhJogc5FI.

WATCH THE VIDEO

Sid Chow Tan:
```
    "These issues changed my life. I
    rearranged my life so I could continue
    to participate and . . . be one of the
    leaders in the movement. I became self-
    employed. I learned skills to be a
    media producer. I learned skills to be
    a community organizer."
```

### Ride for Redress
Gim Wong, a war veteran and son of two head tax payers, was eighty-two years old when he embarked on a cross-country motorcycle ride on July 1, 2004. He wanted to draw attention to the head tax campaign.

Gim Wong:

"The Canadian government has unjustly taken money from my parents and from the Chinese who paid the head tax to enter Canada."

### The Beginning
Margaret Mitchell was the MP for Vancouver East in 1983 when two elderly men requested a refund for their $500 head tax. Dak Mack clutched photocopies of the head tax receipt and his citizenship certificate. Shack Jang Lee had paid the head tax when he arrived in 1918 as a fifteen-year-old. The first to raise the issue in the House of Commons, she sparked a national head tax redress campaign.

### Getting the Word Out
Hanson Lau talked about the head tax on his radio show in Vancouver. Soon, hundreds of people lined up, clutching their head tax certificates.

### Family History Comes to Light
Walter Tom didn't know his grandfather had paid the head tax until he got involved in the redress movement.

▶ Watch Walter Tom discuss his participation in the head tax redress campaign at www.tinyurl.com/rcwheadtax10.

Walter Tom:

"The [old-timers] could hold their heads up high. That was the great thing about the head tax campaign."

WATCH THE VIDEO

# An Official Apology

After twenty-three years of negotiations and six prime ministers, the Canadian government made an official apology and distributed symbolic payments of $20,000 to each head tax survivor and living spouses of deceased payers. Newly elected Prime Minister Stephen Harper fulfilled a campaign promise on June 22, 2006. The government also established a fund for Chinese-Canadian history projects to increase awareness about Canada's past injustices. Two other historic events had furthered the efforts of the head tax redress campaign. In 1988, $21,000 was compensated to Japanese-Canadian survivors of internment during the Second World War. In 2002, New Zealand apologized and provided compensation to head tax payers there. Sadly, less than thirty of Canada's 81,000 head tax payers lived to hear the Canadian government's apology.

**The Oldest Survivor**
Head tax payers, Ralph Lung Kee Lee (right), the oldest surviving head tax payer at age 106, and James Mar (left), aged 94, were in attendance on June 22, 2006 to hear the government's apology first-hand.

**Across Canada by Rail**
The Redress Express was organized as a cross-country train ride for elderly head tax payers and their families to travel to Ottawa to hear Prime Minister Harper's official apology for the head tax.

**Last Spike on Hand**
James Pon holds the last spike, donated by historian Pierre Berton.

 **LISTEN TO THE AUDIO**

Vera Pon:
> "Today, I stand tall with pride as a Canadian of Chinese descent. I finally feel accepted fully as a Canadian. Now I don't feel like a second-rate citizen any more."

🔊 Listen to Vera Pon's reaction to the apology at www.tinyurl.com/rcwheadtax09.

## It's Official

Copies of the apology that was read by the prime minister were given to each head tax payer and surviving spouse. "This government will continually strive to ensure that similar unjust practices are never allowed to happen again."

## Proud Moment

Prime Minister Stephen Harper poses with the head tax payers and surviving spouses holding their copies of the official apology.

## In Tribute

Gim Wong attended in full military uniform, not for himself but for the fathers, grandfathers, and thousands of other Chinese who came to Canada.

Margaret Mitchell:
"I don't think it's fair to families. It doesn't recognize the children and grandchildren."

## Too Late

Walter Tom's grandfather was almost 100 years old when Walter marched in Ottawa during the redress campaign. "He passed away without ever receiving an apology from the government saying that they were sorry for what they have done to him or his generation."

Walter Tom:
"My grand- father, he was proud of the fact that he was involved in the campaign."

Sid Chow Tan:
"The redress is incomplete. Shame on [the government] for . . . leaving the work undone for the affected elderly sons and daughters of head tax families."

**Inclusive Redress**

For many, the campaign is not over. The fight continues for inclusive redress for the sons and daughters of head tax payers.

## Continue the Fight

Charlie Quan's handwritten manifesto calls for the campaign to continue fighting for redress to the descendants of head tax payers.

# Permanent Acknowledgements

All across Canada, memorials, monuments, museums, and other permanent tributes commemorate the contributions of Chinese Canadians. While many were erected several decades ago to remember the railway workers and early Chinatowns, others are more recent. These lasting tributes unlock memories to help in healing the scars of the past, prevent a repeat of past injustices, and open up the darker chapters of Canadian history for the generations to come. The heart-wrenching sacrifices to overcome discrimination and segregation have paved the way for their descendants and all Chinese newcomers, who are now valued as Canadians representing diverse communities. In facing extraordinary challenges, their lives helped to shape Canada.

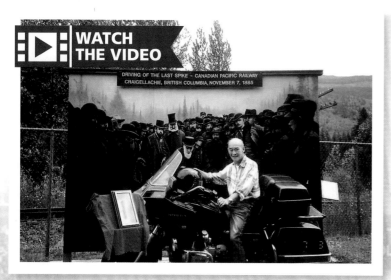

**Last Spike Monument**
During his Ride for Redress across Canada, Gim Wong stopped to visit the Last Spike Monument that marks the site of the driving of the last spike at Craigellachie, BC, in 1885. "The CPR couldn't have been built as the transcontinental railway if it hadn't been for the Chinese," says Canadian historian Pierre Berton.

Watch Pierre Berton talk about the CPR and the hardships of the early Chinese at www.tinyurl.com/rcwheadtax12.

These lasting tributes unlock memories to help in healing the scars of the past, prevent a repeat of past injustices, and open up the darker chapters of Canadian history for the generations to come.

**Railway Monument, Toronto**

Toronto's Memorial to Commemorate the Chinese Railroad Workers occupies a prominent site near the city's train station and railway tracks. Every July 1, a memorial service pays tribute to the workers whose labours united Canada with a ribbon of steel from the Pacific to Atlantic Oceans. Canada's first railway monument was unveiled in 1982 in Yale, BC.

**Railway Monument, Winnipeg**

The Winnipeg Monument to the Chinese Railway Workers was erected in 1997 on the fiftieth anniversary of the repeal of the *Chinese Immigration Act*. Engravings on the bronze Chinese coin depict the history of Chinese immigration. A stone from each province and territory was used in its construction.

Permanent Acknowledgements

**Chinese Railway Monument**
James Pon was the co-founder and chair of the foundation that funded the Chinese railway monument in Toronto.

Sid Chow Tan:
"I think it's about justice. It's about our story. I want generations a hundred years from now to be able to proudly say that our family was a head tax/exclusion family."

**Harling Point Cemetery**
A tradition of the early Chinese was to bury the deceased, exhume the remains after seven years, clean the bones, and ship them to China for final burial in their ancestral cemetery, a practice that continued until the late 1930s. The Harling Point Cemetery in Victoria, BC, is the burial site for over 1,000 Chinese and thirteen communal graves containing unmarked remains that did not get sent to China. It was designated a National Historic Site of Canada in 1996.

Chapter 6: Acknowledging the Past, 1990–2006

### Honouring Railway Workers and Veterans
The Monument to Chinese Railway Workers and War Veterans in Vancouver's Chinatown was erected in 2003. The Chinese character, meaning *Chinese*, is flanked by bronze statues of a railway worker and a Chinese-Canadian soldier. Head tax families are pictured on Canada Day in 2009.

### Canada's 100th Birthday
On January 1, 1967, a special broadcast of Gordon Lightfoot's song *Canadian Railroad Trilogy* was aired nationwide to launch Canada's centennial. The Chinese Community Dancers of Toronto, posing with Governor General Roland Michener and his wife, successfully auditioned for a coveted spot to perform on Parliament Hill in Ottawa on July 1, 1967.

### Commemorative Coins
In 2005, the Royal Canadian Mint released a two-coin commemorative set on the 120th anniversary of the completion of the CPR. One coin depicts a train on a rail bridge over the Fraser River, the other features the Memorial to Commemorate the Chinese Railroad Workers. Both coins have the image of her Majesty Queen Elizabeth II on the other side.

Permanent Acknowledgements

**Head Tax Monument, St. John's**

The Chinese Head Tax Monument was unveiled in St. John's, Newfoundland, in 2010 as part of a larger project to provide an online exhibit and educational resources about the head tax and the contribution of the early Chinese in the province, like those featured in the monument's 1940 photograph of the Chinese community.

**History in Photos**

The Newfoundland and Labrador Head Tax Redress Organization unveiled this large wall artwork in 2010 as part of a mural project in St. John's. The drawings are based on several historical photographs, including one of the Hop Wah Laundry in 1922.

**Mash Up**

A hip-hop mash-up, entitled "Our Story," was created by brothers Trevor and Matt Chan as a tribute to the families affected by the head tax and exclusionary period. Based in Vancouver, No Luck Club is an instrumental hip-hop group. Their great-grandfather paid the $500 head tax and their great-grandparents were forced to live apart due to the *Chinese Immigration Act*. "It's what we're about. It's our history."

Trevor Chan:

"Some friends whose parents came to Canada . . . back in the seventies or eighties, from mainland China or Hong Kong . . . have no idea what went down."

**Soul by Tracks**

The visual artworks of Judi Michelle Young, daughter of a head tax payer, draw inspiration from her family history. This piece, entitled *Soul by Tracks,* represents the building of the railway and the Chinese workers who died during its construction. Judi is the first Chinese-Canadian president of the Sculptors Society of Canada.

**Family Stories**

*Our Canadian Stories* is a photo exhibition produced by the Chinese Canadian National Council to highlight family stories about the head tax. Many projects like this one have been developed with grants from the federal government's Community Historical Recognition Program.

Permanent Acknowledgements

# EPILOGUE: CHINESE CANADIANS

# A Multicultural and Multiracial Society

Chinese newcomers are still arriving from all provinces of China and from around the world, each with their own language, culture, and unique histories: Hakka Chinese from Jamaica; ethnic Chinese from Vietnam; Hokkien from Taiwan; and so on. Hong Kong was the largest source of immigrants in the 1990s, then it was outranked by China in the 2000s. People of Chinese ancestry in Canada number over 1.3 million, over 85 per cent of whom live in Toronto, Vancouver, Montreal, Calgary, and Edmonton. After English and French, Cantonese and Mandarin are the most-widely spoken languages in Canada.

**HELP SAVE CHINATOWN**

Attend City Hall Meeting
June 16th. 1969 8 P.M.

保存華埠 挽救華埠 籲賴須要 參加六月十六日晚上入時市政廳會議

**New Money Saves Chinatown**
Two-thirds of Toronto's Chinatown was torn down for the construction of a new city hall and public square. The Save Chinatown Committee launched a campaign in 1969 to prevent further demolition. Since the 1970s, investors from Hong Kong and China have revitalized Chinatowns across Canada with new businesses, professional services, and residential developments.

**Fighting the Wrecker's Ball**
In the 1950s and 1960s, Chinatowns across Canada were threatened with redevelopment and Chinese communities rallied to fight the bulldozer. While some, like Montreal's Chinatown, underwent a sharp decline in size and population after the Second World War, others were relocated or demolished.

## At the Top

Patrick Chan is a three-time world champion, two-time silver-medal Olympian, and six-time Canadian champion in figure skating. Other outstanding athletes include Olympian gold-medal wrestler Carol Huynh; badminton champion Michelle Li; Olympic gold-medal rhythmic gymnast Lori Fung; Quene Yip, BC Sports Hall-of-Famer; Norman Kwong, first Chinese-Canadian professional football player; and, Larry Kwong, first Chinese-Canadian hockey player in the NHL.

# . . . no limit to what Chinese Canadians can do . . .

### Accomplishments in All Areas

There is no limit to what Chinese Canadians can do and accomplish. They are domestic workers and restaurateurs as much as they are doctors, engineers, and business people. Sook-Yin Lee is a Canadian broadcaster, musician, actor, filmmaker, and former *MuchMusic* VJ. She is the host of CBC Radio's *Definitely Not the Opera*.

### Representing all Canadians

Chinese Canadians are active participants in all levels of the political arena. Adrienne Clarkson was the first Asian-Canadian governor general. David Lam, Norman Kwong, and Philip Lee have served or are serving as lieutenant-governors; Vivienne Poy (pictured above), Lillian Dyck, and Victor Oh as senators.

A Multicultural and Multiracial Society

## Moving to the Burbs

As Chinese Canadians moved away from inner-city Chinatowns, they set up their residences and businesses in the suburbs. Some call these areas Chinatowns while others call them ethnoburbs. Forty-five per cent of the residents of Richmond, B.C., are Chinese, the highest rate in the country. Asian-themed shopping centres, like the Dragon Centre in Toronto, proliferated despite the tension that often erupted between developers and long-time local residents.

## Gateway into Victoria's Chinatown

By the 1970s, heritage neighbourhoods became the focus for revitalization. Chinatowns were regarded as vibrant destinations that welcomed everyone. The Gate of Harmonious Interest, one of many traditional gateways erected across the country, welcomes visitors in Victoria. Its Chinatown, the oldest surviving one in Canada, is a National Historic Site.

## Coat of Arms

Family associations, like the Wong Association, are still active today, although their role in providing settlement, employment, housing, and financial services has shifted to a mostly social purpose. *Wong* is the seventh most popular surname in China and there are 39 million Wongs around the world. In 2011, the Wongs were the first Chinese in Canada to have a coat of arms.

## Racing the Dragon

Dragon boat racing, steeped in ancient Chinese tradition that dates back thousands of years, is the fastest growing water sport in the world. Chinese and non-Chinese alike participate in dragon boat festivals and races. It is an example of the acceptance and integration of Chinese culture into Canadian life.

Epilogue: Chinese Canadians

**Performing Arts**
Even with the popularity of Chinese television, movies, and DVDs, the love of Chinese opera has endured with performances by local and visiting opera troupes.

Judi Michelle Young: "[My mother] loved Chinese opera and taught herself to read and write Chinese from the opera LPs. I could name all the famous actors."

**Winnipeg's Chinese Cultural Centre**
Chinese cultural centres, like this one in Winnipeg, promote cultural exchanges and serve as a focal point for community activities.

**Calgary's Chinese Cultural Centre**
The Calgary Chinese Cultural Centre features a twenty-metre-high ceiling, modelled after the Temple of Heaven in Beijing.

**Toronto's Chinese Cultural Centre**
The Chinese Cultural Centre of Greater Toronto opened in 1998 as the largest cultural centre in North America.

**Asian Heritage Month**
The month of May is designated as Asian Heritage Month in Canada and the US. Festival Accès Asie in Montreal is one of ten Canadian festivals that promote artists from over twenty Asian countries.

**Colourful Stamps**
Canada Post issues annual commemorative stamps featuring Chinese New Year, like the Year of the Dragon, and, most recently, the gateways that grace Chinatowns across the country.

A Multicultural and Multiracial Society

# Timeline

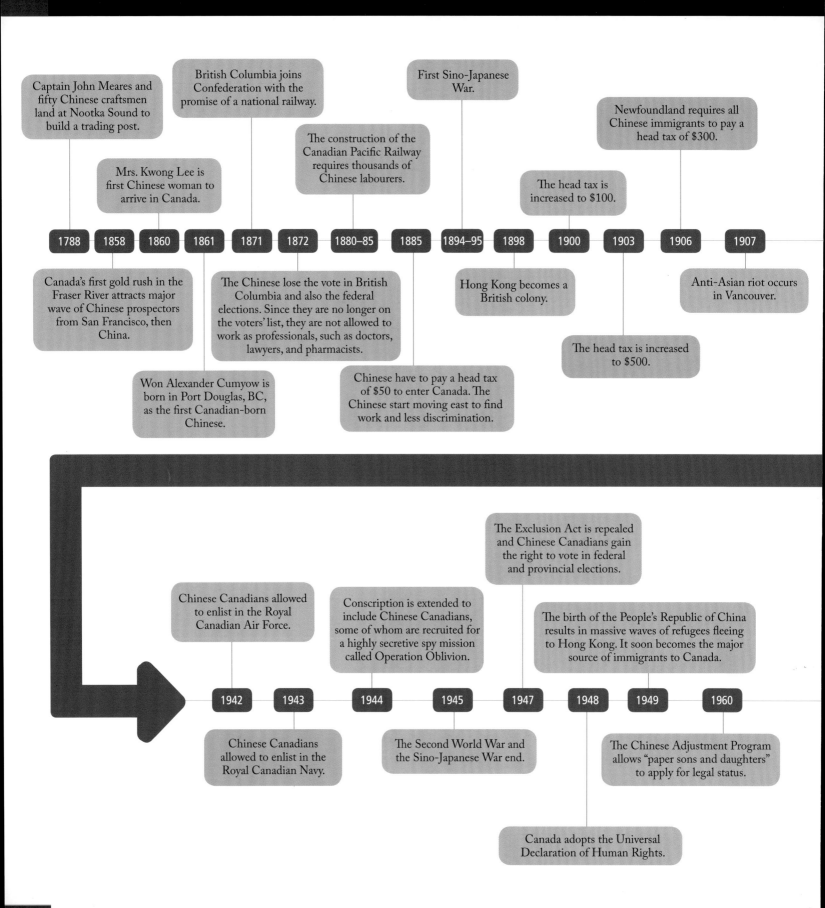

Captain John Meares and fifty Chinese craftsmen land at Nootka Sound to build a trading post.

British Columbia joins Confederation with the promise of a national railway.

First Sino-Japanese War.

Newfoundland requires all Chinese immigrants to pay a head tax of $300.

Mrs. Kwong Lee is first Chinese woman to arrive in Canada.

The construction of the Canadian Pacific Railway requires thousands of Chinese labourers.

The head tax is increased to $100.

**1788  1858  1860  1861  1871  1872  1880–85  1885  1894–95  1898  1900  1903  1906  1907**

Canada's first gold rush in the Fraser River attracts major wave of Chinese prospectors from San Francisco, then China.

The Chinese lose the vote in British Columbia and also the federal elections. Since they are no longer on the voters' list, they are not allowed to work as professionals, such as doctors, lawyers, and pharmacists.

Hong Kong becomes a British colony.

Anti-Asian riot occurs in Vancouver.

The head tax is increased to $500.

Won Alexander Cumyow is born in Port Douglas, BC, as the first Canadian-born Chinese.

Chinese have to pay a head tax of $50 to enter Canada. The Chinese start moving east to find work and less discrimination.

The Exclusion Act is repealed and Chinese Canadians gain the right to vote in federal and provincial elections.

Chinese Canadians allowed to enlist in the Royal Canadian Air Force.

Conscription is extended to include Chinese Canadians, some of whom are recruited for a highly secretive spy mission called Operation Oblivion.

The birth of the People's Republic of China results in massive waves of refugees fleeing to Hong Kong. It soon becomes the major source of immigrants to Canada.

**1942  1943  1944  1945  1947  1948  1949  1960**

Chinese Canadians allowed to enlist in the Royal Canadian Navy.

The Second World War and the Sino-Japanese War end.

The Chinese Adjustment Program allows "paper sons and daughters" to apply for legal status.

Canada adopts the Universal Declaration of Human Rights.

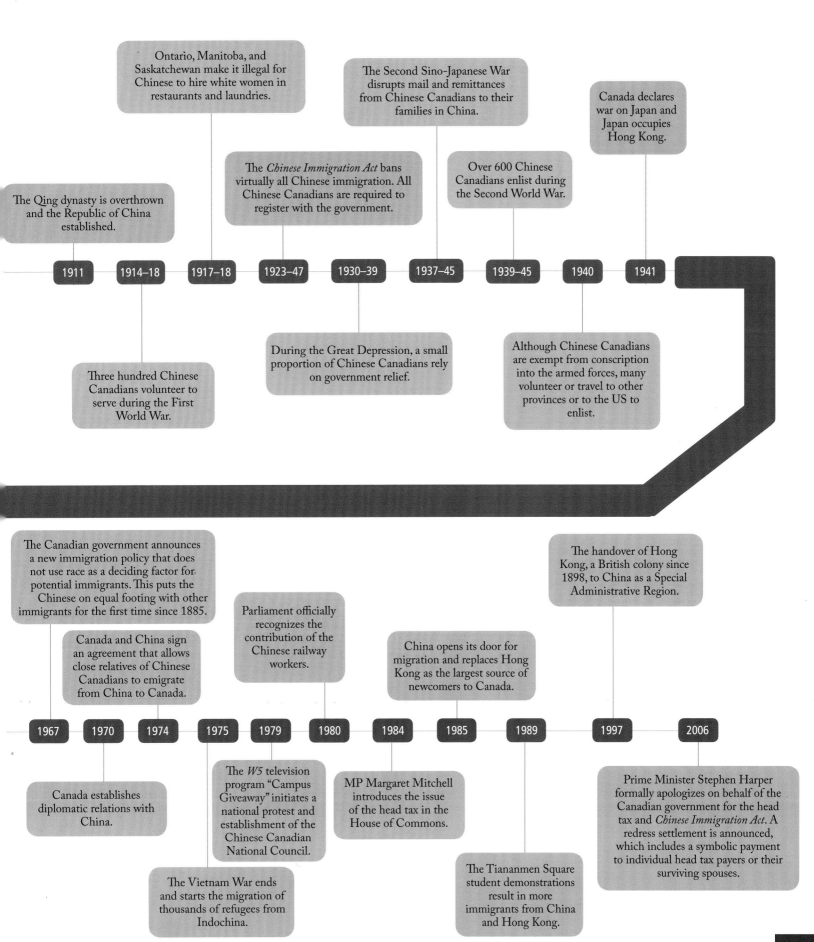

Ontario, Manitoba, and Saskatchewan make it illegal for Chinese to hire white women in restaurants and laundries.

The Second Sino-Japanese War disrupts mail and remittances from Chinese Canadians to their families in China.

Canada declares war on Japan and Japan occupies Hong Kong.

The *Chinese Immigration Act* bans virtually all Chinese immigration. All Chinese Canadians are required to register with the government.

Over 600 Chinese Canadians enlist during the Second World War.

The Qing dynasty is overthrown and the Republic of China established.

| 1911 | 1914–18 | 1917–18 | 1923–47 | 1930–39 | 1937–45 | 1939–45 | 1940 | 1941 |

During the Great Depression, a small proportion of Chinese Canadians rely on government relief.

Although Chinese Canadians are exempt from conscription into the armed forces, many volunteer or travel to other provinces or to the US to enlist.

Three hundred Chinese Canadians volunteer to serve during the First World War.

The Canadian government announces a new immigration policy that does not use race as a deciding factor for potential immigrants. This puts the Chinese on equal footing with other immigrants for the first time since 1885.

The handover of Hong Kong, a British colony since 1898, to China as a Special Administrative Region.

Parliament officially recognizes the contribution of the Chinese railway workers.

Canada and China sign an agreement that allows close relatives of Chinese Canadians to emigrate from China to Canada.

China opens its door for migration and replaces Hong Kong as the largest source of newcomers to Canada.

| 1967 | 1970 | 1974 | 1975 | 1979 | 1980 | 1984 | 1985 | 1989 | 1997 | 2006 |

Canada establishes diplomatic relations with China.

The *W5* television program "Campus Giveaway" initiates a national protest and establishment of the Chinese Canadian National Council.

MP Margaret Mitchell introduces the issue of the head tax in the House of Commons.

Prime Minister Stephen Harper formally apologizes on behalf of the Canadian government for the head tax and *Chinese Immigration Act*. A redress settlement is announced, which includes a symbolic payment to individual head tax payers or their surviving spouses.

The Vietnam War ends and starts the migration of thousands of refugees from Indochina.

The Tiananmen Square student demonstrations result in more immigrants from China and Hong Kong.

Timeline

# Glossary

**Amnesty:** A general pardon issued by the government for past offences.

**Bachelor:** An unmarried man.

**Buddhism:** The teachings of Buddha and his followers, who spread the word of enlightenment and peace. It is one of China's main religions and the world's fourth largest, with 360 million followers.

**Cannery:** A business that cans food for retail sale. Many Chinese immigrants worked in canneries in BC.

**Cantonese:** Chinese dialect spoken mostly in Guangdong province, Hong Kong, and Macau; also refers to the people and style of Chinese cooking from Guangdong.

**Chain migration:** When an individual or family immigrated to Canada, other members of their village or extended family members typically followed them.

**Citizenship:** The country that a person belongs to. When you are a citizen of a country, you can have a passport from the country and receive all its rights and benefits.

**Civil rights:** The basic privileges that come with being a member of society in a given country. The right to vote, have an education, and receive justice in the courts are all civil rights.

**Communism:** A political movement that aims to create an equal social order based on common ownership and distribution of material wealth based on need and where everyone works for the common good.

**Compensation:** The payment of money to make up for a wrong that was done

to a person or group. For Chinese Canadians who had paid the head tax or their surviving spouses, the compensation of $20,000 was a symbolic payment to acknowledge the hardships caused by the head tax.

**Confucianism:** A philosophy based on the teachings of Confucius, who was a major influence on the political, social, and cultural life of China.

**Conscription:** A government policy that required all able-bodied men eighteen years of age and older to join the military and fight in the war.

**Culture:** The customs, traditions, and values of a country or its people.

**Daoism:** A philosophy based on the teachings of Laozi. It promotes a simple life that fits into the natural flow of events.

**Delegation:** A small group of people who represent a much larger group's ideas or demands.

**Democracy:** A government by the people, exercised either directly or through elected representatives.

**Dialect:** A form of language spoken in a particular region or group. The Chinese language has hundreds of dialects, such as Cantonese and Hakka.

**Discrimination:** Unjust actions that are caused by a particular mindset or prejudice; a means of treating people negatively because of their group identity. Discrimination may be based on age, ancestry, gender, language, race, religion, political beliefs, sexual orientation, family status, physical or mental disability,

appearance, or economic status. Acts of discrimination hurt, humiliate, and isolate their victims.

**Dynasty:** A historical period of rulers from the same family.

**Emigration:** Leaving one's home country to go to a different country.

**Franchise:** The right to vote. Chinese Canadians were denied the franchise in provincial elections in BC and Saskatchewan and in federal elections until 1947.

**Gold Mountain:** The Chinese term for North America.

**Gold rush:** Sudden migration of people to an area where gold has been found

**Great Depression:** A time between 1930 and 1939 when Canada experienced a long-term downturn in economic activity.

**Gum Shan:** See Gold Mountain.

**Guomindang:** A political party founded by Sun Yat-sen in 1912. Also known as the Nationalist Party.

**Han:** The main ethnic group of China, constituting over 90 per cent of the population.

**Head tax:** A fixed fee charged for each Chinese person entering Canada. Implemented in 1885 at $50, it was raised to $100 in 1900, and $500 in 1903.

**Heritage:** Traditions passed down to younger generations.

**Immigration:** The arrival of people into a country from their homeland.

**Injustice:** A wrongful action taken against an individual or group that denies them of their basic rights.

*Loh wah kew:* A Cantonese phrase referring to elderly Chinese immigrants.

**Mainstream:** The values and traditions of the majority.

**Manchus:** The people who came from Manchuria and established the Qing (or Manchu) dynasty (1644–1911) in China.

**Mandarin:** The official language of China.

**Matchmaker:** Someone who arranges marriages.

**Middle class:** A social, economic, and cultural grouping usually composed of business, professional, and skilled people.

**Nationalist Party:** See Guomindang.

**Paper son or daughter:** A young Chinese male or female who entered Canada with identity papers that were bought for them.

**Prejudice:** An attitude, usually negative, directed toward a person or group of people based on incorrect or distorted information. Prejudiced thinking may result in acts of discrimination.

**Prospector:** A person who searches for gold or other precious metals.

**Racism:** A belief that one race is superior to another. People are not treated as equals because of their cultural or ethnic differences. Racism may be systemic (part of institutions, governments, organizations, and programs) or part

of the attitudes and behaviour of individuals.

**Redress:** To right a wrong, sometimes by compensating the victim or by punishing the wrongdoer. Refers to the movement within the Chinese-Canadian community for an official apology and payment for the injustices of the government's head tax and the *Chinese Immigration Act.* For many Chinese Canadians, the redress movement will continue until compensation is extended to the surviving children of head tax payers.

**Refugees:** People who leave a country for fear of persecution based on race, religion, political opinion, or nationality.

**Registration:** A person is required to report to an authority and give his or her name, place of residence, and other personal information, and it is kept on record. All Chinese Canadians, whether born in Canada or not, were required to register with the government within two years of the enactment of the *Chinese Immigration Act in* 1923.

**Segregation:** The policy or practice of separating people of different races, classes, or ethnic groups, especially as a form of discrimination.

**Social assistance:** Money provided by the government to help out people who are in poverty.

**Traditions:** The cultural rituals, customs, and practices of a particular country, people, family, or institution handed down over a long period of time.

**Values:** Beliefs that are considered important by an individual or a culture.

**Victory Bonds:** Certificates sold by the Canadian government to help pay for the First and Second World Wars.

**Warlord:** A person with power who has both military and civil control due to armed forces.

# For Further Reading

Books/Novels:

Wong, David H. T. *Escape to Gold Mountain: A Graphic History of the Chinese in North America*. Vancouver: Arsenal Pulp Press, 2012.

Yee, Paul. *Blood and Iron: Building the Railway*. Toronto: Scholastic Canada, 2010.

Non-Fiction Books:

Burney, Shehla. *Coming to Gum San: The Story of Chinese Canadians*. Toronto: D. C. Heath Canada Limited for the Multicultural History Society of Ontario, 1995.

Harris, Heather, and Mary Sun. *The Chinese Canadians*. Scarborough: Nelson Canada, 1982.

Yee, Paul. *Chinatown: An Illustrated History of the Chinese Communities of Victoria, Vancouver, Calgary, Winnipeg, Toronto, Ottawa, Montreal and Halifax*. Toronto: James Lorimer, 2005.
_____. *Struggle and Hope: The Story of Chinese Canadians*. Toronto: Umbrella Press, 1996.

Films:

*Etre Chinois au Québec (Being Chinese in Quebec)*. 2013. Productions Multi-Monde. 70 min. Documentary film examines the Chinese in Quebec from a youth perspective.

*From C to C: Chinese Canadian Stories of Migration*. 2011. Simon Fraser University. 46 min. An award-winning documentary about the impact of the head tax and Chinese Immigration Act on Chinese Canadians, including Sid Chow Tan and Charlie Quan. Excerpts viewable online at www.sfu.ca/fromctoc/.

*In the Shadow of Gold Mountain*. 2004. NFB. 43 min. The stories of the last survivors of the head tax and Chinese Immigration Act. Viewable online at www.nfb.ca/film/in_the_shadow_of_gold_mountain.

*Lost Years*. 2011. Lost Years Production, Inc. 90 min. Kenda Gee retraces three generations of family history that includes his grandfather who paid the head tax. Radio personality Hanson Lau and Second World War veteran Gim Wong are also featured.

Websites:

chinesecanadian.ubc.ca/about — Chinese-Canadian Stories: Uncommon Histories from a Common Past.

chrp.library.ubc.ca — Chinese Canadian Stories.

www.collectionscanada.gc.ca/eppp-archive/100/205/301/ic/cdc/generations — Across the Generations: A History of the Chinese in Canada.

www.collectionscanada.gc.ca/chinese-canadians/ — The Early Chinese Canadians, 1858–1947.

www.vpl.ca/ccg — Chinese-Canadian Genealogy.

Audio and Video Clips:
Albert Lee
www.mhso.ca/chinesecanadianwomen/en/database.php?c=71

Germaine Wong
www.mhso.ca/chinesecanadianwomen/en/donor.php?d=Wong,%20Germaine

Gim Wong
www.youtube.com/watch?v=wOIMHVsqp1A

James Pon
www.mhso.ca/tiesthatbind/JamesPon.php

Judi Michelle Young
www.mhso.ca/chinesecanadianwomen/en/donor.php?d=Young,%20Judi%20Michelle

Sid Chow Tan
www.youtube.com/watch?v=k9EhJogc5FI

Vera Pon
www.mhso.ca/chinesecanadianwomen/en/donor.php?d=Pon,%20Vera

Walter Tom
www.roadtojustice.ca/video/walter-tom

Other Books by Arlene Chan:

*Awakening the Dragon: The Dragon Boat Festival*. Toronto: Tundra Books, 2004.

*The Chinese Community in Toronto: Then and Now*. Toronto: Dundurn Press, 2013.

*The Chinese in Toronto from 1878: From Outside to Inside the Circle*. Toronto: Dundurn Press, 2011.

*The Moon Festival: A Chinese Mid-Autumn Celebration*. Toronto: Umbrella Press, 1999.

*Paddles Up! Dragon Boat Racing in Canada*. Toronto: Dundurn Press, 2009.

**WATCH THE VIDEO**

Look for this symbol throughout the book for links to video and audio clips available online.

**Visit www.lorimer.ca/wrongs to see the entire series**

Additional books, films, websites, and videos are listed in the Resources section of the Righting Canada's Wrongs series website at www.lorimer.ca/wrongs

# Visual Credits

Acces Asie: p. 87 (bottom left)

Berton, Pierre. *The Great Railway Illustrated.* Toronto: McClelland & Stewart, 1972: p. 22 (bottom)

B.C. Archives: p. 32 (top left, E-02768); p. 51 (middle, e_06997)

Burney, Shehla. *Coming to Gum San.* Toronto: D.C. Heath Canada, 1995: p. 73 (bottom)

California State Library: p. 13 (bottom, DAG-0102)

Canada Post Corporation 2012. Reproduced with Permission: p. 87 (bottom right)

Chan, Anthony: p. 72 (top left and bottom)

Chan, Francis: p. 83 (top left)

Chan, Trevor: p. 83 (top right)

Chateaigneau, Gerard: p. 85 (top)

Chinese Canadian National Council: p. 74 (both); p. 75 (bottom right); p. 77 (top right and bottom); p. 80–81; p. 83 (bottom right)

Chinese in Northwest America Research Committee: p. 41 (bottom)

Chiu, Tam Kam: p. 86 (top)

Choi, Kelvin: p. 87 (middle right)

Chou, Wynnie: p. 36 (top); p. 38 (bottom), p. 57 (bottom right); p. 60 (top right); p. 61 (top)

City of St. John's Archives: p. 48

City of Toronto Archives: p. 25 (bottom, Fonds 1268, Series 1317, Item 379A); p. 56 (bottom, Fonds 1244, Item 1682)

Doug Chin Collection: p. 36–37; p. 39 (top); p. 65 (top)

Earl Lock Collection: p. 56 (top)

Glenbow: p. 17 (middle, NA-4088-1); p. 70 (bottom, PA3852-1)

Goldsborough, Gordon: p. 78–79

Government of Canada: p. 26–27; 27; 43 (top); 52 (top right); p. 71 (top right)

Harvey, John: p. 86 (middle)

Huang, Annian, compiler. *The Silent Spikes.* China International Press, 2006: p. 81 (bottom)

Jean Lumb Collection: p. 52 (top left); p. 67 (bottom); p. 69 (bottom); p. 71 (top left); p. 72 (top right); p. 81 (right)

K. Dock Yip Collection: p. 44 (left)

Kwan, Cheuk: p. 72 (middle); p. 73 (top)

Lee, Albert: p. 46 (top right and top left); p. 53 (middle); p. 55 (bottom); p. 63 (top); p. 68 (bottom)

Lew, Mavis: p. 70 (top)

Li, Julia Ningyu. *Canadian Steel, Chinese Grit.* Paxlink Communications, 2000: p. 24 (top); p. 46 (bottom); p. 59 (middle); p. 67 (top); p. 80 (top left)

Library and Archives Canada: p. 14 (top, PA-125990); p. 15 (top, C-064765; bottom, PA-053604); p. 16 (bottom, PA-172888); p. 17 (bottom, PA-118156); p. 19 (top right, PA-025136; bottom, 7883); p. 20 (left, C-72064); p. 21 (top, C-050449; middle, 3089); p. 22 (top, C-151855); p. 24 (middle, 3402474); p. 25 (bottom, C-003-693); p. 28 (3943); p. 32 (top right, PA-118195; bottom, 122688); p. 35 (top, 3192435); p. 36 (PA112287); p. 45 (bottom, PA-085998); p. 49 (top, PA-087321); p. 51 (bottom, C-068863); p. 59 (bottom, PA-211880); p. 60 (top left) 9201259-V6); p. 62 (middle, C-046350)

Library of Congress: p. 8 (left, USZ62-64593; right, 10966-3), p. 9 (top, USZ62-102718; left, USZ62-56119; right, USZ62-68807), p. 10 (top USZ-25833; middle, USZ62-68807); p. 11 (USZ62-56123); p. 12 (bottom, W7-844); p. 17. (top, LC-UCZ62-93788); p. 18 (right, USZ62-14976); p. 23 (top, USZ62-120580; bottom right, USZ62-120604); p. 39 (USZ62-42598); p. 40 (middle, USZ62-6487); p. 49 (bottom, 2a14454u); p. 50 (USZC4-12563); p. 51 (top right, USZ62-87729); p. 52 (bottom, USZ62-118816); p. 60–61 (top, USZC4-12168); p. 62 (top, USZ62-132048)

Little Pear Garden Collective: p. 87 (top)

Lock Family Collection: p. 63 (bottom)

Lumb, Edward: p. 79

Mah, Daniel and Valerie: p. 40 (top); p. 54 (left); p. 55 (top right), p. 57 (bottom left); p. 71 (bottom right and bottom left)

Meares, J. *Voyages Made in the Years 1788 and 1789 from China to the Northwest Coast of America*: p. 12 (top)

Mills, Edward: p. 80 (bottom right)

Mitchell, Margaret: p. 75 (middle)

Multicultural History Society of Ontario: p. 45 (middle), Mary Ko Bong Collection, Film 5-10); p. 47 (bottom, CWimageG8); p. 69 (top left)

Newfoundland and Labrador Head Tax Redress Organization: p. 82 (top right)

Ng, William: p. 86 (bottom)

Oakland Museum of California: p. 14 (bottom)

Poy, Neville: p. 85 (middle)

Qiao, Shan: p. 76 (all); p. 77 (middle left)

Quance, Jeff: p. 53 (bottom)

Royal BC Museum, BC Archives: p. 31 (top, Image A-04437); p. 33 (bottom, Image D-00410); p. 34 (Image C-09748); p. 37 (Image C-07944)

Tan, Sid Chow: p. 24 (bottom); p. 46 (middle); p. 47 (top); p. 69 (middle left and middle right); p. 77 (bottom left)

Tom, Walter: p. 75 (bottom left); p. 77 (middle right)

*Toronto Star*: p. 40 (bottom, Oct 11, 1901)

Treasury Board of Canada Secretariat: p. 77 (top left)

United Church of Canada Archives: p. 41 (middle)

University of California, Berkeley, Bancroft Library: p. 13 (top, 0499A)

University of British Columbia, Chung Collection: p. 33 (middle); p. 51 (top left, 25056)

Vancouver Archives: p. 29 (AM358; CVA 153-2); p. 32 (middle, A25206-141); p. 41 (top right, AM571-S4; CVA 287-3); p. 53 (top, Am571-S4; CVA 287-8); p. 56 (middle, A45341); p. 57 (middle, AM54S4; BUN 157.1); p. 60–61 (bottom, A03709)

Vancouver Public Library: p. 19 (top left, 19540); p. 20 (right, 78423); p. 23 (bottom left, 12866); p. 25 (top, 389); p. 30 (3653); p. 33 (top, 6729); p. 36 (middle, 13114); p. 41 (top left, 50111); p. 42 (939); p. 43 (bottom, 136); p. 45 (top left, 86658; top right, 39046); p. 67 (top, 8799A); p. 66 (top, 41618b)

Van Son, Brendan: p. 16 (top)

Verney, Peter: p. 59 (top left)

Veterans Affairs Canada: p. 64

Waddington, Alfred. *The Fraser Mines Indicated*: p. 18 (left)

Wikipedia: p. 31 (bottom); p. 38 (top)

Wing None Eng Collection: p. 61 (bottom); p. 69 (top right)

Wong Family Association: p. 86 (middle left)

Wong, David H.T. *Escape to Gold Mountain.* Vancouver: Arsenal Pulp Press, 2012: p. 10 (bottom)

Wong, Gim: p. 55 (left); p. 59 (top right); p. 75 (top); p. 78

Wong, Hank: p. 58 (both); p. 62 (bottom); p. 63 (middle)

Wong, Tony: p. 87 (centre)

Wright, Miriam: p. 82 (top left); p. 82 (bottom)

Xie, Elwin: p. 54 (right)

Yee, Paul. *Chinatown.* Toronto: James Lorimer, 2005: p. 25 (middle); p. 44 (right); p. 65 (bottom); p. 66 (bottom); p. 73 (middle); p. 84 (both); p. 85 (bottom left); p. 87 (middle left)

Young, Judi Michelle: p. 21 (bottom); p. 47 (middle); p. 68 (top); p. 83 (middle)

Zvonar, John E.: p. 80 (bottom left)

# Index